Praise for *Remembering the Light Within*

*"I love this book. I want to give it to everyone. It is the owner's manual for egos that have forgotten they are souls."*
— **Richard Barrett**, author of
*A New Psychology of Human Well-Being: An Exploration of the Influence of Ego-Soul Dynamics on Mental and Physical Health*

*"This is truly a book for our times; a handbook of awakening to the Light within. Ron and Mary Hulnick are two of the most accomplished spiritual teachers of our time. They are love itself—the real deal. While more than 5 thousand students have graduated from their celebrated programs out of the University of Santa Monica, now we can all partake of their practical, life-changing wisdom."*
— **Joan Borysenko, Ph.D.**, *New York Times* best-selling author of *Minding the Body, Mending the Mind*

*"I've known Ron and Mary for more than 30 years and have watched their work grow and mature over time. Not only are they a class act but also their work is truly exceptional. I am inspired every time I meet one of their graduates.* Remembering the Light Within *is filled with the wisdom of the ages. It is truly a life-changing book."*
— **Jack Canfield**, co-author of the Chicken Soup for the Soul® series and *The Success Principles*™

*"The liberating wisdom in this book radiates and flows from each page. No one will read it just once. This book is not just a one-time experience but rather a gateway to the timeless in us all."*
— **Steve Chandler**, author of *Time Warrior: How to Defeat Procrastination, People-Pleasing, Self-Doubt, Over-Commitment, Broken Promises and Chaos*

"Remembering the Light Within *is an inspiring guide for the discovery of our innate wisdom and inner knowing. Mary and Ron Hulnick are masters in helping individuals understand that our greatest potentials do not have to be acquired or manufactured anew, but only realized. This book is an essential guide for anyone seeking deeper meaning and fulfillment. This awareness is crucial not just for the individual seeking it; it is essential, at this point in history, for our flourishing and continuance as a species on our beloved planet."*

— **Larry Dossey, M.D.**, author of *One Mind: How Our Individual Mind Is Part of a Greater Consciousness and Why It Matters*

*"I wish to thank Mary and Ron Hulnick for producing another masterpiece. They guide us step-by-step through some very powerful techniques and mind-sets. The idea is to free us from harmful thought habits, and teach us precious skills to live more consciously and happily. When we are on the journey to become what we really are, all knowing is remembering, all realizations are discoveries of what we have always known but what, in the intricate pathways of our lives, we so easily forget."*

— **Piero Ferrucci**, author of *Your Inner Will: Finding Personal Strength in Critical Times*

*"Ron and Mary Hulnick's new book is a treasure trove of wisdom for today's spiritual seekers. Not only is the book filled with liberating insights, it is also grounded in practical processes that bring spirituality to light in your daily activities.* Remembering the Light Within *is a book to read and re-read often to awaken and nurture your spiritual essence."*

— **Gay Hendricks, Ph.D.**, author of *The Big Leap* and co-author of *Conscious Loving Ever After*

*"Reading* Remembering the Light Within *is like taking a course in soul-based living. It takes you by the hand and, in a most pragmatic way, leads you home to your Spiritual Self."*

— **Leonard Laskow, M.D.**, author of *For Giving Love: Awakening Your Essential Nature Through Love and Forgiveness*

# REMEMBERING
## THE
# LIGHT
## WITHIN

# ALSO BY MARY R. HULNICK, PH.D., AND H. RONALD HULNICK, PH.D.

*Financial Freedom in 8 Minutes a Day:*
*How to Attract and Manage All the Money You'll Ever Need*

*Loyalty to Your Soul: The Heart of Spiritual Psychology**

*Available from Hay House

Please visit:

Hay House USA: www.hayhouse.com®
Hay House Australia: www.hayhouse.com.au
Hay House UK: www.hayhouse.co.uk
Hay House South Africa: www.hayhouse.co.za
Hay House India: www.hayhouse.co.in

# REMEMBERING THE LIGHT WITHIN

A Course in Soul-Centered Living

## Mary R. Hulnick, Ph.D.
## H. Ronald Hulnick, Ph.D.

**HAY HOUSE, INC.**
Carlsbad, California • New York City
London • Sydney • Johannesburg
Vancouver • New Delhi

*Published and distributed in the United States by:* Hay House, Inc.: www.hay house.com® • *Published and distributed in Australia by:* Hay House Australia Pty. Ltd.: www.hayhouse.com.au • *Published and distributed in the United Kingdom by:* Hay House UK, Ltd.: www.hayhouse.co.uk • *Published and distributed in the Republic of South Africa by:* Hay House SA (Pty), Ltd.: www.hayhouse.co.za • *Distributed in Canada by:* Raincoast Books: www.raincoast.com • *Published in India by:* Hay House Publishers India: www.hayhouse.co.in

*Project editor:* Nicolette Salamanca Young • *Cover design:* Lenore Perry
*Interior illustrations:* Courtesy of Drs. Ron and Mary Hulnick
*Interior design:* Riann Bender

Poem on pg. xviii is reprinted as it appears in *The Essential Rumi* (new expanded edition), translations by Coleman Barks. HarperCollins Publishers: New York, NY, 2004. Copyright © 2004 by Coleman Barks. Used with his permission.

Poem on pg. 46 is from the Brason-Sargar publication: *Life Is the Way It Is.* Copyright © 1978 and 1980 Sondra Anice Barnes. Used with her permission.

Quote on pg. 99 is from *A Course in Miracles*©, (T-16.IV.6:1), from the second edition, published in 1992, and is used with permission by the publisher and copyright older, the Foundation for Inner Peace, P.O. Box 598, Mill Valley, CA 94942-0598, www.acim.org and info@acim.org.

The authors of this book do not dispense medical advice or prescribe the use of any technique as a form of treatment for physical, emotional, or medical problems without the advice of a physician, either directly or indirectly. The intent of the authors is only to offer information of a general nature to help you in your quest for emotional, physical, and spiritual well-being. In the event you use any of the information in this book for yourself, the authors and the publisher assume no responsibility for your actions.

**Cataloging-in-Publication Data
is on file with the Library of Congress**

Tradepaper ISBN: 978-1-4019-4976-1

10 9 8 7 6 5 4 3 2 1
1st edition, February 2017

Printed in the United States of America

SUSTAINABLE
FORESTRY
INITIATIVE

Certified Sourcing
www.sfiprogram.org
SFI-01268

SFI label applies to text stock only

# INVOCATION

Lord of all Creation, we call ourselves forward into your Light and Loving, and we ask that everyone reading this book be cleared, filled, surrounded, and protected by the pure Light of Living Love. We ask that only that which is for the Highest Good of all concerned be brought forward. And at this time we ask that Spirit place a Blessing with you, the reader:

*The Blessing of an Open Heart,*
*The growing Awareness of Your Essential Loving Nature,*
*The willingness to Awaken into the Love that you are,*
*and*
*The Courage to Remember the Light Within.*

*So be it.*

✦ ✦ ✦

# CONTENTS

# FOREWORD

Ron, Mary, and I are sitting in the Green Room, backstage at Royce Hall at the University of California, Los Angeles (UCLA). We are drinking tea and munching on sandwiches, dressed in our graduation robes complete with tassels. The hall is nearly full now; over 1,700 people have gathered to celebrate the graduation of 250 students who have completed programs in Spiritual Psychology at the University of Santa Monica (USM). Ron and Mary are hosting the ceremony in their joint role as founding faculty and co-directors of USM, and I am here to give the commencement speech.

I am struck by how calm Ron and Mary are. This is the biggest day in their calendar. There's no offstage anxiety—only genuine excitement for what is about to unfold. "This is a day of great joy," says Mary, who is radiant and in soft focus. "Indeed it is," says Ron, as he takes her hand. Ron and Mary often hold hands; it's how they are with each other. Faculty, staff, the official photographer all pop in and out of the Green Room as we converse. Everyone is focused, happy, and on purpose.

"We are not human beings with souls; we are souls who are having a human experience—that's what we teach our students," Ron tells me. He speaks with conviction. His words are fresh. They are like living water from a spring—not still water from a pot.

Ron looks deep into me and says, "Imagine what sort of world we would live in if everyone knew they are not just a body, but a creative, infinite soul."

In my commencement speech, I share a story from my book *Shift Happens!* I'd been 26 years old, and an Indian guru had looked deep into me, just like Ron had, and asked, "Who are you?" I told him my name, and he smiled. "Who are you?" he repeated. I told him that I was a writer. His smile just became broader. "Who are you?" he asked again. I panicked. I told him what I thought he wanted to hear. "I'm a soul," I said. The guru didn't buy it. He laughed uncontrollably. He didn't ask again, but his kind eyes stayed fixed on me. Sitting there, I had what Ron and Mary call a Soul moment, and I came alive to myself.

"Our Spiritual Psychology Programs are first and foremost a Spiritual experience," Mary tells me. "We don't want our students only to write essays about the Soul. We want them to know their Authentic Self. Everything we offer—our programs, our online events, and our books—is designed to help people call in the Light and have a direct experience of Soul-Centered Living."

Ron and Mary have hosted 35 USM graduation ceremonies so far. More than 5,000 students have graduated from one of their spiritual programs, including the Master's in Spiritual Psychology, the Certificate in Soul-Centered Living, and the Certificate in Soul-Centered Professional Coaching. And in this new book, *Remembering the Light Within: A Course in Soul-Centered Living*, Mary and Ron have synthesized many of their teachings into a Spiritual workbook—a songbook, as they call it—that will help you to tune in to the melody, harmony, and lyrics of your Soul.

I spoke with Mary and Ron a number of times during the writing of *Remembering*. The way they wrote this book together was a teaching in itself. They called in the Light and made themselves into instruments for what their Souls most wanted to teach. At one point, they rewrote the structure of the book to allow for a new flow. They updated chapters continuously as they each experienced new insights, and they road tested all the practical exercises to be sure that each one is a fresh and relevant offering.

I am so happy that *Remembering* exists. And I am happy for you that you now hold it in your hands. I encourage you to read it slowly. Savor and absorb the wisdom, and, above all, do the exercises and assignments. *Remembering* is not just Spiritual entertainment! It's a practice-based workbook designed to help you experience a *holy shift* from believing you are an ego in a body to realizing you are a Soul in the Universe. Imagine that! Imagine being grounded fully in your unconditioned Self, sharing your Soul gifts with us all and living a truly Soul-Centered Life.

*Remembering the Light Within* is an invitation from Ron and Mary's Hearts to yours: to inhabit your Soul nature even more fully and to share your Soul-Song, which only you can sing, with the world.

— Robert Holden,
best-selling author of *Life Loves You*,
*Holy Shift!*, and *Authentic Success*

❖ ❖ ❖

# INTRODUCTION

If you're reading this Introduction, you may be asking, "This title is compelling and I'm experiencing myself being drawn to it. I'm very curious to know what you mean by *Remembering the Light Within: A Course in Soul-Centered Living*. It sounds so invitational and intriguing—even a bit mysterious and unconventional. I'm wondering: What do these words mean? And is this for someone like me?"

And further, you may be saying, "I want a life filled with Meaning, Purpose, and Fulfillment—a life that helps me understand and truly *know* who I am and why I am here. Do *Remembering the Light Within* and *Soul-Centered Living* have anything to do with answering my deepest questions and fulfilling my Heartfelt yearnings—the things that truly matter to me most? Can they help me live an inspired life?"

Our answer is a wholehearted and enthusiastic "Yes!"

For more than 30 years, we have provided students with opportunities for learning and applying life-changing Principles and Practices of Spiritual Psychology. You may be asking, "What is Spiritual Psychology? What are these Principles and Practices? Can they help alleviate the mental anguish and emotional suffering I experience at times? Can they assist me in transforming my consciousness and my life?"

Again we say, "Yes. That is *exactly* what they're designed for!"

If you delve deeply into the meaning of the word *psyche*, you'll find phrases such as "breath, principle of life, soul." But if you explore the meaning of the word *psychology*, you'll find, "the science of mind and behavior." Somehow, in the translation from essence to practice, the most important aspect of "psyche" has been lost. We recognize our Calling as restoring the Spiritual dimension to the Heart of an authentic psychological inquiry. It is this reintegration that is the Heart of a truly Spiritual Psychology, which we define as the study and practice of Conscious Awakening.

And what does Awakening mean? It begins with the awareness that we simultaneously reside in two worlds. The one we are most aware of is known as physical world reality. It's the world of our every day existence with which we are familiar and which we think of as the "*real* reality." It is the world we know through our five senses.

However, there is another reality beyond five-sense reality that is multidimensional and spiritual in nature. For our purposes we define Awakening as waking up into this "other" reality, where we experience the Awareness of our Essential Spiritual Nature as Loving, Peaceful, Joyful, Free, Enthusiastic, Beautiful, Creative, Wise, and more! The Persian poet and mystic, Jalaluddin Rumi, is certainly speaking from an Awakened state when he wrote:

The breeze at dawn has secrets to tell you.
    Don't go back to sleep.
You must ask for what you really want.
    Don't go back to sleep.
People are going back and forth across the doorsill
    where the two worlds touch.
The door is round and open.
    Don't go back to sleep.

Awakening into the Awareness of who you truly are and living your life from within that Awakened state is the essence of Soul-Centered Living. As the evolutionary tide is rising and larger numbers of people are Awakening to the Awareness that they are, in fact, Divine Beings having a human experience, the Principles and

Practices of Spiritual Psychology provide the context and tools for living into that Awareness. It is, in fact, your destiny to Awaken; for as you do so, you are actually Remembering that which is and always has been true.

This book could be considered your personal experiment in what we speak of as "the Michelangelo effect" which was so brilliantly expressed by the master sculptor himself when he said, "I saw the angel in the marble and carved until I set him free." In just such a way, the process of Remembering is not so much a journey of "becoming." It is a process more akin to removing layers of veils from the lens of your perception, thus revealing the "angel" that is the essence within each of us.

Now here's what to us is the most interesting and exciting part. This process of Remembering is not primarily a meditative process, though we encourage a spiritual practice we refer to as Spiritual Exercises. Awakening is a very active process through which step-by-step you remove or dissolve the barriers from your consciousness that are all that prevent you from knowing your Soul's nature—from experientially knowing that you are the Presence of Love. Can you imagine walking through this world in a consciousness that is Awake to Love? Wouldn't that be Amazing Grace?

As you participate with the material in this book, you will be doing the work that you came to this earth to do. And in so doing you will be liberating yourself to live in an Awakened state in ever-increasing Awareness that you are a Soul using this human experience to truly know yourself as the Presence of Love.

And why do we entitle this book *Remembering the Light Within*, as if to imply that somehow you've forgotten something you previously knew? In our experience, we all suffer from greater or lesser degrees of "Spiritual amnesia." We've forgotten who we are and why we're here. People attracted to this work very often experience themselves being called to it. It's as if they hear a note that resonates with a deep inner knowing. Perhaps they pick up on a piece of information such as the foundational Principle of Spiritual Psychology: We are not human beings with a Soul; we are Souls using a human experience for the purpose of remembering our Essential Nature is Loving. Or, perhaps they've had a mystical experience that Awakened them into the Awareness that there's more going on here than can be explained within the confines of five-sense reality.

One final note on what we mean by the word *Light*. Recently in a class during an opening meditation, I (Mary) seemingly misspoke. Rather than saying, "Gently close your eyelids . . ." I said, "Gently close your eye lights." After we all laughed, I realized that what I had said was actually very accurate. Eyes are often considered windows to the Soul, and when we look into each other's eyes we see the Light within. You see the Light of God emanating through another as a reflection of the Living Love that is within your Self—and is your true nature. So when we speak of the Light Within, we are not speaking metaphorically. We are speaking rather experientially. We recognize this quality when we make statements to the effect of someone having a "glow" around them or a "sparkle" within them.

And so, when we speak with words such as Light, Awakening, Remembering, Enlightenment, Spirit, God, and whatever words you might use to describe that level of consciousness, we have an intention. It is our deepest prayer that through the use of this book, you will have inner experiences of Remembering the Light Within—Remembering that you are the Presence of Love—and move forward Living a Soul-Centered Life—your unique and beautiful life of Meaning, Purpose, and Fulfillment.

It is with deep Gratitude in our Hearts and our many years of experience applying the Principles and Practices of Spiritual Psychology in our own daily lives while also supporting students in learning to do the same, that we share this book with you. It is our intention to provide you with inspiration, encouragement, practical tools, and opportunities for learning how to live into the Spiritual Context—to experientially know that you are a Soul and that your life serves a Spiritual purpose. That is Soul-Centered Living.

### Ways You May Use This Book

If this book were a song, it would be a beautiful Love Song—music and messages that open your Heart and are in deep resonance with your Soul's Essential Nature. Like a song, there is a beginning and an ending, with a melody that is written in such a way that it continually unfolds as you surrender yourself to experiencing the music through the 26 chapters. And like all music that touches the Heart, the more you give yourself to it, the more it inspires you, and the more beautiful it becomes. And before you know it, you are the Love Song no longer waiting to be sung.

We've carefully designed this book so that its use tends to result in ongoing experiences of more deeply Awakening into greater Awareness of your Authentic Self. And we highly recommend keeping a journal as you progress, since it will provide a chronicle of your experiences that then act as supportive reference points. It's a wonderful way to record the shifts in Awareness you are making and to anchor and integrate your transformation.

Each chapter consists of the following elements:

- Information that is simultaneously inspirational and life changing.

- Stories and quotes designed to inspire and affirm you in the process of Remembering through coming into greater resonance with your Essential Nature.

- A Practice or Practices designed to present opportunities to apply and experience the benefits of using the Principles and Practices of Spiritual Psychology. As you work with them inside yourself and in your everyday life, they are intended to foster experiences of Awakening into the Awareness that you are the Presence of Love.

- An intention related to the material that you can energize, enliven, and activate by speaking it from your Heart and/or contemplating it and its relevance to you and your life.

- Suggestions for journal entries designed for you to record the awareness and shifts you are making as you progress through the book. This provides a chronicle of your experiences, which then become supportive reference points and wonderful ways of anchoring and integrating the transformation you are experiencing.

Some people prefer to simply read a book and garner the information; if that method works well for you, we support you in using it. However, we suggest that you consider the following approach for a deeper experience.

Read one chapter at a time and then engage with the Practice(s) and intention at the end of the chapter for a period of time—perhaps for a week or two—before moving on to the next chapter. The approach of working with the material over time is one many people experience as very empowering, supportive, and transformative. Seeing as the information and tools contained within this book are sequential and cumulative, this approach supports you in gaining experience with the Principles and Practices of Spiritual Psychology as well as practical grounded ways for you to integrate them into your everyday life.

By virtue of its use, the book becomes a resource and guidebook for Soul-Centered Living and Remembering who you are. The Practices are not things you do once or twice and then move on. They are powerful and empowering, and when utilized regularly over time, become integrated as a Way of Being. And if your experience is anything like that of the thousands who have gone before you, you'll likely be using them for the rest of your life.

You have our Love and encouragement in Remembering and living into the fullness of the Loving that is inside of you. In your Soul, you're already Awake to the Love that you are! This book is intended as both inspiration and support for Awakening into that Awareness and living a Soul-Centered Life—an inspired life filled with Love, meaning, and purpose.

✤ ✤ ✤

**Authors' Note:** Throughout this book, there are many capitalized words that wouldn't normally be treated in this way. We've chosen to capitalize these words because they are direct references to the Authentic Self—in this way, we are distinguishing them from words used to reference the ego level. Our intention is for you, the reader, to recognize the capitalized words as Authentic Self qualities.

CHAPTER 1

# ENTERING THE SPIRITUAL CONTEXT

*"We are not human beings having a spiritual experience.*
*We are spiritual beings having a human experience."*
— Pierre Teilhard de Chardin

What does it mean to be a Spiritual Being having a human experience? Might it be that Teilhard perceived most people as seeing themselves in exactly the opposite way? Perhaps he was aware that many of us tend to define ourselves as human beings who occasionally, if we're fortunate, have a spiritual experience. We tend to think of ourselves as having several dimensions, one of which is spiritual. But what does life look like if we perceive it from his perspective?

Teilhard's quote is a powerful statement regarding the Spiritual Context—the Awareness that you are a Soul and that your life serves a Spiritual purpose—for it opens a portal to another way of perceiving yourself, your life experiences, and your purpose for being on this earth in human form.

Our journey into the Spiritual Context begins by distinguishing between what we refer to as the Goal Line and Soul Line of life. Both are important to understand, as many people are simply unaware of these two dimensions.

### *The Goal Line of Life*

The Goal Line of Life refers to physical-world reality—the stage upon which you play the starring role in the adventure that is your life.

In physical reality, your primary vehicles for navigating the world are your mind, which thinks things through and evaluates what you see; your emotions, which feel your experiences as another way of receiving information; and your behavior, which shows how you take action, produce results, and receive feedback from the Universe. You utilize feedback to maintain or alter your course as you pursue your goals.

You use your mind, emotions, and behavior (along with your five senses of sight, sound, touch, taste, and smell) to navigate toward success—as you define it. The underlying assumption is that the more you move into the positive, the happier and more fulfilled you will be. This is because everything is perceived in terms of polarity; life is lived as a continuum with so-called negative experiences on the one extreme and positive experiences on the other. Within this perspective, your life will largely consist of continually striving for more and more positive experiences, as defined in terms of success in the physical world. For example, earning as much as you can and being as successful as possible are goals you can easily spend an entire lifetime pursuing.

You can probably relate to this way of evaluating your experiences because it likely matches the way you've been taught, conditioned, or programmed to perceive the world and your place within it. Utilizing this dualistic way of thinking and seeing, you make plans, measure your success, and even determine the worthiness and value you place upon yourself based on your progress in achieving your goals. Hence we refer to this orientation in the world as the Goal Line of Life.

$(-)$ ⟶ $(+)$

Physical World Reality
The Goal Line of Life

## Moving Beyond the Goal Line of Life

A rapidly increasing number of people are realizing that material achievements alone may not be a sufficient yardstick for measuring their success in life. They are considering the possibility that the quality of their inner experience throughout their life is at least equally essential, if not more essential, to living a fulfilling life.

In fact, the larger cultural conversation has expanded into explorations of authentic success, which is excellently expressed in the words of professional life coach Robert Holden: "All the happiness, success, health, and abundance you experience in life comes directly from your willingness to love and be loved." In his book *Authentic Success*, he urges self-reflection: "If your definition of success has little or no measure of love in it, get another definition." When you begin moving into an Awareness of authentic success, you find yourself considering the possibility that Spiritual Awakening has relatively little to do with how successful you are in physical-world reality.

For most of us Awakening at this time, Spiritual Awakening often has a great deal to do with the degree to which you experience your life as fulfilling. In fact, more and more people are aware of experiencing a deeper yearning. So many find themselves asking questions such as: "Is this all there is?" "Isn't there more to life than this?" "Who am I?" "What is my purpose?" "How can I experience greater meaning and fulfillment in my life?" and "How can I make a more meaningful contribution and live a more fulfilling life?"

These are all excellent questions, answers to which are revealed to you as you experience your own process of Awakening.

## The Soul Line of Life

You may be asking, "Just what is the process of Awakening?" Awakening does not take place externally in physical-world reality, although the benefits of Awakening can definitely be experienced on the Goal Line of your life. Rather, Awakening occurs internally within each person as a process—an ongoing, unending series of experiences and awareness. We refer to the dimension within which Awakening occurs as Spiritual Reality, or the Soul Line of Life. It operates relatively independently from, yet in harmony with, the Goal Line of Life.

The Soul Line of Life has been addressed by every one of the world's major spiritual traditions as well as spiritual teachers, mystics, and sages throughout recorded history. All such teachings have in common the notion of a Unified Consciousness, or Awareness, that is the Essence of all that exists. This "Unified Consciousness" is usually referred to as God, or Spirit, but any name you would choose to refer to this essential "Something" will do just fine. It's what German physicist Max Planck, who won the Nobel Prize in Physics in 1918, was talking about when he said in a 1931 interview for *The Observer*: "I regard consciousness as fundamental. I regard matter as derivative from consciousness. We cannot get behind consciousness. Everything that we talk about, everything that we regard as existing, postulates consciousness."

Further, there is widespread agreement as to the nature or essence of this "Something"; and to us, the word that best describes this essence is *Love*. So it is not surprising that all the world's great spiritual traditions agree that ascending into greater levels of Love is what their life's path or journey is primarily about. Where spiritual traditions differ is in their notions of how to get there—not in where they are going.

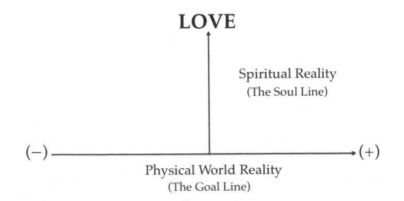

**LOVE**

Spiritual Reality
(The Soul Line)

(−) ————————————————→ (+)

Physical World Reality
(The Goal Line)

## *Spiritual Psychology: Entrance into the Spiritual Context*

The realization that Awakening is an inner process that can be nurtured and encouraged is what inspired us to bring forward the Principles and Practices of what we refer to as Spiritual Psychology. As we discussed in the Introduction, it is a way of reintegrating the Spiritual dimension into the essence of psychological inquiry. It is the study and practice of the art and science of Conscious Awakening: learning how to identify, recognize, and navigate within the context of a "Spiritual Being having a human experience."

Spiritual Psychology contains 33 Principles (see Appendix A) as well as many Practices we have discovered to be foundational and facilitative to the process of Conscious Awakening. The following three Principles provide entrance into the Spiritual Context.

**1. God, Universal Consciousness, whatever name suits you, comprises all that exists.**

This means that there can be nothing existing outside of this consciousness.

**2. The nature of God is Unconditional Love.**

This means that the essential nature of all that exists is Unconditional Love in exactly the same way that the essential nature of gravity is to assure that you remain on the ground and don't go floating off into space. Love, like gravity, acts on everyone equally.

**3. Since we are all a part of God, our Essential Nature is also Love—and we have the opportunity of knowing our Loving nature experientially, here and now.**

This means that, at the core of their being, each and every person who exists, has ever existed, or will ever exist—whether or not they realize it or demonstrate it behaviorally—is an inherently Loving Being.

## *The Inherent Nature of Conscious Awakening*

While many seekers will accept the Principles of Spiritual Psychology as part of the process to Awaken, there is an inherent challenge. Due to our indoctrination into a Goal Line orientation to life, it's tempting to think of the process of Awakening as one of becoming more Loving. Thus, we try to turn the process of Spiritual Awakening into a Goal Line project, which is one focusing on achievement. However, it is impossible for you to become a more Loving person. You can't become what you already are—a Divinely inspired Loving Being. So what can you do?

**You can become more and more *aware* of, and *awake* to, your inherent Loving nature!**

Indeed, the process of Spiritual Awakening is nothing less than becoming more and more aware, experientially, of your Loving Essence. As you Awaken and become more and more aware of your Essential Loving Nature, your attitudes and behavior automatically become less critical, judgmental, controlling, righteous, or blaming—and instead become more kind, caring, Joyful, Creative, and Compassionate. People who notice your shift might think that you've become a more Loving person, but the truth is that you are simply behaving more in harmony with your inherently Loving Nature.

This brings us to the nature of Awakening. It's important to understand that Awakening is an ongoing process that continuously takes place over periods of time—with rare exceptions, such as the Indian sage Ramana Maharshi, who Awakened at age 16. It is also a totally experiential process. Think of swimming: You can read about swimming, including instructions on how to swim, but until you get into the water and begin experiencing the process, you will never really "know" what swimming is. Awakening is like that.

As author Henry Miller said, "The Buddhas and the Christs are born complete. They neither seek love nor give love, because they are love itself. But we who are born again and again must discover the meaning of love, must learn to live love as the flower

6

lives beauty." It is with this Awareness in mind and Heart that we offer this book to you: an invitation into the Spiritual Context. Come into the Healing and liberating waters of Awakening—and Remembering the Light Within.

## THIS CHAPTER'S PRACTICES

You will find two Practices in this chapter: a meditation and a journaling exercise. For the following meditation, as with any of the meditations in this book, you may find it helpful to record it. Some people like to record these meditations in their own soft voice, while others prefer to have someone with an especially soothing voice record them. Neither way is better, it's just a matter of what works best for you. Save your meditations on a mobile device so you can take a time-out whenever you choose and play one—the more often the better.

### Meditation for Entering the Spiritual Context

*Center your Awareness in your Heart with the intention of entering the Spiritual Context . . .*

*We invite you in the Sacred Silence to consider and reflect on Henry Miller's words: "The Buddhas and the Christs are born complete. They neither seek love nor give love, because they are love itself. But we who are born again and again must discover the meaning of love, must learn to live love as the flower lives beauty."*

*Consider what it means to you to live Love . . . Perhaps it's as simple as being present in this moment, following the rising and the falling of your breath . . .*

*Take a few moments now to contemplate the three Principles that provide entrance into the Spiritual Context: The nature of God is Unconditional Love . . . Repeat that phrase silently inside . . . The nature of God is Unconditional Love . . .*

*Next, inwardly repeat, "I am a Soul having a human experience"*
*. . . I am a Soul having a human experience . . .*

*And now consider this . . . As a Divine Being, my Essential Nature*
*is Love . . . And repeat silently . . . As a Divine Being, my Essential*
*Nature is Love . . .*

*Receive of the Peace that is present as you relax in the radiant*
*warmth of the Loving that is your Essence.*

When you feel complete, write a few notes in your journal
about your experience, then do the Practice below.

### Sentence Completion Practice

We invite you to take some time to consider the material presented in this chapter and your experience during the guided
meditation. Copy the following stem sentences, along with your
responses, in your journal now.

- If God (or Universal Consciousness or whatever name
  suits you) comprises all that exists, then . . .

- If the nature of God is Unconditional Love, then . . .

- If my Essential Nature is also Love, then . . .

**Note:** There's no need to limit your answers. As you are
moved to do so, write as many responses to each stem sentence as
you are able.

## INTENTION

I am Awakening into the fuller Awareness of my inherently
Loving Nature, Joyfully living my life knowing that I am
an emanation of the Divine.
of my inherently Loving nature and to live my life
knowing that I am an emanation of the Divine.

# CHAPTER 2

# THE POWER OF CLEAR INTENTION

*"Enthusiasm is one of the most powerful engines of success. When you do a thing, do it with all your might. Put your whole soul into it. Stamp it with your own personality. Be active, be energetic, be enthusiastic and faithful, and you will accomplish your object. Nothing great was ever achieved without enthusiasm."*

— RALPH WALDO EMERSON

Take Emerson's powerful, inspiring Call to Heart, and move forward on both the Goal Line and Soul Line of your life with enthusiasm! To start, you'll need to formulate and align with your own intentions for Awakening.

Let's clarify here what we mean by *intention*. Intention is perhaps best understood as determination to act in a certain way or to produce a specific outcome. It can also be thought of as your resolve. One of the best examples we're aware of is your body's intention to breathe. If you'd like to experience the power of intention now, try holding your breath for, say, 10 minutes.

Most people can't hold their breath for more than 30 seconds, and even highly conditioned athletes are generally gasping for air after two minutes. Well-known exceptions to this are certain pearl divers, who have been known to hold their breath for as long as seven minutes as they descend to depths of over 100 feet to scoop up exceptional pearls of luminous luster.

And while you continue holding your breath, consider the following: Luster is the amount of light a pearl reflects from both its surface glow and the deep mirrorlike reflection of its inner light. The better the quality of the pearl, the more superior its luster.

Now take a deep breath. Good! If you had any doubts regarding intention, you quickly saw that no matter how hard you might try, at some point your body will start breathing all by itself. The body's intention to breathe is innate and compelling—not to be denied!

Another intention that is inherent within you, regardless of the degree to which you are aware of it, is your intention to Awaken to the Luminous Light and Lustrous Love that is your Essential Nature. In fact, if you didn't have that intention, you wouldn't be reading this book.

You may be wondering, "What does an intention to Awaken really mean? And why does it matter? What difference will it make? Does it have any practical value? Will my intention to Awaken help me have better relationships with those close to me? Will I feel better about myself? Will I experience myself as more resourceful in responding to the challenges that are part of a human life? And perhaps most important of all, will it also assist me in learning ways I can experience more Meaning, Purpose, and Fulfillment in my life—and will I experience more Love?"

We trust that you will discover your own positive answers to all these questions as you progress through this book.

## *You Are a Creator*

Our words, and the amount of energy with which we infuse them, are expressions of our intention. As such, they are a primary medium through which we create our life. The Spiritual Psychology Principle of Intention states: In your Universe, your word is your law; thus, the power of intention. This powerful statement is an admonition to be truly conscious of what we say because every word we speak, whether conscious or unconscious, is an intention with which we are creating our lives.

That's right. Your current life is a manifestation of your cumulative intentions, whether you think you have any or not! Unclear or competing intentions tend to result in nebulous outcomes. When you focus on what you want to avoid rather than focusing on what you intend to create and experience, it can program limitation, lack, and negative outcomes into your life. You must hold the picture of your desired outcome in your mind, positively affirm it with your words, and move toward it. Remember that negative affirmations spoken unconsciously will create more of what you don't want; they are one of the ways you unintentionally sabotage yourself.

### What Is a "Clear" Intention?

Clear, positive intention involves clarity of purpose and the willingness to act on it.

As Abraham Lincoln said, "Always bear in mind that your own resolution to succeed is more important than any other one thing." When you hold a clear intention, your thoughts, feelings, and behaviors—including your words—align. As you align your purpose, choices, words, and actions with the outcomes you wish to experience or manifest, you initiate inner alignment with the Essence of who you are—a Divine Being having a human experience!

It is empowering to clarify your intention. You not only begin to engage in actions that propel you forward in harmony with your intention, but also you experience the taking of dominion within your own consciousness, which results in inner and outer cooperation. In truth, in your world, your word is law. Thus, you experience the empowerment that comes from clear, positive intention.

When engaging in the process of setting clear intentions, be aware that there are different kinds, depending upon whether you are focusing on the Goal Line or the Soul Line. The following medieval tale is one of our favorite stories to clarify the distinction between Goal Line and Soul Line intentions:

A traveler came to a work site and saw two men carrying stone. One man was working listlessly with a sullen expression on his face, while the other man was cheerfully singing as he busily carried stone after stone.

"What are you doing?" asked the traveler of the sullen worker.

"Laying stone,'" was his reply.

The traveler asked the same question of the industrious worker.

"Building a cathedral," he replied.

This is intention at work.

### Goal Line Versus Soul Line Intentions

Goal Line intentions are all about aligning your thoughts, feelings, and behavior in service to achieving tangible results in areas of your life such as relationships, finance, health, work, and service. Soul Line intentions are more aspirational in nature. They are directly connected to your attitudes, choices, and resolve related to Awakening. Soul Line intentions are an expression of a deeper yearning that is in harmony with the evolutionary impulse moving both within you and on the planet.

When creating intentions on the Goal Line in physical-world reality, your intentions tend to be focused on goals and aspirations such as:

- My intention is to increase my income by 20 percent or more this year.

- My intention is to manifest a heartfelt relationship leading to marriage and family.

- My intention is to have a child within the next two years.

- My intention is to express my creativity artistically in ways that bring me alive!

- My intention is to take my supplements each day in support of my health and well-being.

On the other hand, when creating intentions on the Soul Line, your intentions look more like the following:

- My intention is to Awaken to the Loving that is my Essential Nature.

- My intention is to see myself, others, and the world through Soul-Centered eyes—the eyes of my Heart.

- My intention is to remember the Light within and live a more Soul-Centered Life.

- My intention is to fully participate in practices that foster and nurture my Awakening.

- My intention is to sacrifice and surrender the barriers within me that have blocked me from the Awareness of my Self as a Soul having a human experience.

It's important to note that these are *all* valid intentions. After all, quality of life on the Goal Line is important.

Here's an example of intention in action on the Goal Line. Consider someone who struggled with alcohol addiction but has just accomplished a year of sobriety. Their intention has resulted in choices that have produced the desired result. In other words, there is an alignment between their thoughts (the clarity of their vision—"I am releasing my addiction to alcohol"), their emotions or feelings ("I feel confident and empowered living my life as a sober person), and their behavior (cessation of drinking alcohol). In our experience, the alignment of these three almost always results in success.

## Keys for Formulating Clear, Positive Intentions

The following steps are your keys to formulating clear, positive intentions:

- Center yourself in your Heart.

- Distinguish Goal Line intentions from Soul Line intentions. Recognize which intentions are concerned with results in physical-world reality and which have to do with your Awakening.

- Be specific while remaining open to the greater good. In other words, ask for what you want while knowing that Spirit always responds in accordance with your Highest Good.

- State your intention(s) in the positive. (No "Get rid of . . ." or "I don't want . . .")

- In your creative imagination, visualize the outcomes as if they are already present. Focus on clear pictures of your intentions already made manifest.

- Let go of attachment to the outcomes; trust in the Divine. This is a beautiful opportunity for practicing high involvement and low attachment to an outcome. Our experience is that when your intention is clear, the methods appear.

- Hold your intentions in the following context: This or something better for the Highest Good of all concerned.

- Remember, your words are your wand! Perhaps one of your intentions is that your thoughts, feelings, and actions are in alignment with your intentions.

As you clarify, align, formulate, and act upon your positive intentions, you'll naturally find your consciousness elevating, and you will be living your life at a new level—in the Joy, Aliveness, Creativity, Enthusiasm, Peace, Freedom, and Loving of your Authentic Self.

## *An Intention in Action*

The book you are reading is the result of an intention that I (Mary) expressed in a meeting with some staff. I was talking with our Director of Online Education about how to support members of the University of Santa Monica's online community in more deeply anchoring and integrating the Principles and Practices of Spiritual Psychology. Together we birthed the idea for an offering of inspirational messages and activities that would be engaging and supportive for the community. We named it 33 Days of Awakening Through Loyalty to Your Soul.

Then the fun began! Soon thereafter, I was awakened very early one morning with a strong inner knowing that I was to arise and begin writing. I arose early for the next 45 days, formulating a series of inspirational messages and activities for the USM Online community. When the first offering was almost complete, I spoke with USM's Director of Online Education and a consultant who works with the University. "I loved writing the messages. Sharing with our community was great! *And* I want to write for more people." Unbeknownst to myself, that statement was the declaration of a powerful intention!

A couple of weeks later, Ron and I found ourselves having dinner with Arianna Huffington and her sister, Agapi, both of whom we've known for many years. Conversation was lively and included updating each other on our creative endeavors. When I mentioned 33 Day of Awakening, both women expressed enthusiasm for the program and the desire to see it. Arianna expressed an interest in offering it to a segment of the *Huffington Post* audience.

Fast-forward to a little less than three months later, and the program was being shared with more than 17,000 *Huffington Post* readers from all 50 states plus 138 countries around the world! From there, Ron's and my vision shifted to expanding the material and writing this very book.

Remember: Within Peace, Acceptance, Non-Attachment, and Love, there is a profound Awareness that compels you toward the fulfillment of your purpose. When you act upon that Awareness, you discover your intention to Awaken unto Love. That process will likely take you beyond your comfort zone and may involve what seem like deep dives into previously unchartered waters. Venturing beyond the familiarity of your comfort zone supports you in your transformation and eventual revelation of the lustrous pearl of your luminous Self.

### THIS CHAPTER'S PRACTICES

*Clarify Your Intentions*

Formulate one set of intentions for yourself pertaining to the Goal Line (your physical-world reality) and another set for the Soul Line (Spiritual Awakening). You may also want to come up with an Overarching Spiritual Intention: a primary intention for your life. You'll find an example below.

Write your intentions in your journal. You may want to reference them now and again, and add to, modify, or delete some of your intentions. (We find that intentions tend to clarify and refine as we grow spiritually.)

Remember that Goal Line intentions concern tangible results in your physical life, while Soul Line intentions relate to your attitudes, choices, and resolve related to Awakening; however, both sets of intentions are valid. For example:

**My Goal Line Intentions:**

- My intention is to engage in more meaningful employment.
- My intention is to make some new friends.

### My Soul Line Intentions:

- My intention is to make a meaningful contribution in this world.

- My intention is to live my life in ways that are an expression and reflection of the Peace, Compassion, and Loving that are the essence of my Spiritual nature.

### My Overarching Spiritual Intention:

- My Overarching Spiritual Intention is to fully Awaken Spiritually, living in the Awareness that I am a Soul having a human experience, and that I am the Presence of Love, living a surrendered life serving Spirit's intention.

## *Place Your Intentions into the Light*

Regularly review your Goal Line, Soul Line, and Overarching Spiritual Intentions, then place them into the Light for the Highest Good. This is a powerful Practice that can be done daily. The following prayer is one way you can approach this:

"Father Mother God, just now I center myself in my Loving Heart. I ask for your Guidance and Assistance. My deepest prayer is to be used as an instrument of your Light, Love, and Healing Grace. Here are my Goal Line intentions and my Soul Line intentions. *[Read them here.]* Know that my Overarching Spiritual Intention is to fully Awaken Spiritually and to know myself as the Presence of Love, living a surrendered life serving Spirit's intention for me. With Gratitude, I place my intentions into the Light for the Highest Good, knowing that I am Loved and Blessed."

## INTENTION

I am enthusiastically clarifying and acting upon
both my Goal Line and Soul Line intentions in service to my
Awakening and living the life of my Heartfelt dreams.

# CHAPTER 3

# SEEING THE LOVING ESSENCE WITHIN YOURSELF

*"And now here is my secret, a very simple secret.*
*It is only with the heart that one can see rightly;*
*what is essential is invisible to the eye."*

— ANTOINE DE SAINT-EXUPERY

Two of the original core Principles of Spiritual Psychology are: "We are not human beings with Souls; we are Souls having a human experience," and "Our Essential Nature is Love." As we've delved more deeply into the Principles and Practices of Spiritual Psychology, we've come to recognize that it is more accurate to say that we are Souls *using* a human experience. Using it for what purpose? For Awakening, Remembering, or becoming more and more conscious of our Essential Loving Nature.

This chapter's focus is designed to support you in strengthening your Awareness of the Precious Presence of who you truly are: a Soul having a human experience, whose Essential Nature is Love. Why is this important? Because, if you're like most people, you've learned to relate with yourself with conditional Love—usually contingent on unrelenting standards of perfection.

Think about the last time you heard a harsh, judgmental, critical voice inside your head saying that you or the things you did weren't good enough. Consider how transformational and liberating—yes, even game changing—it can be to cultivate a different way of being, relating, and communicating with yourself. The information that we share next is designed to provide context that can open the door to a gentler, kinder, more Compassionate, and nurturing way of relating with your Self.

## The Reality of the Ego Versus the Authentic Self

Within Spiritual Psychology, we draw a distinction between two centers of awareness, the ego/personality, or small self, and the Authentic Self or Soul. To comprehend and operate within both physical-world reality and the Spiritual Context, it's helpful to know how both the ego and the Authentic Self function in your consciousness.

The ego is composed primarily of your mind and emotions. Your mind consists of all your thoughts, attitudes, and beliefs; some of these are deeply held and form the foundation or matrix upon which you construct the framework of reality you use to navigate your life. It is your mind that reasons, thinks things through, and evaluates according to what you believe to be so. Righteousness and judgmental thoughts or words tend to be hallmarks of egotistical thinking rather than Authentic Self expressions.

Your emotions, or feelings, utilize the information produced by your mind; they are your thoughts felt physiologically. They are a source of energy through which you take action in the physical world. Your emotions are a reflection of your thoughts and beliefs; as such, if someone does something to violate an important belief of yours, you will likely feel strong emotions toward them. For example, if I believe taxes are too high, I'll feel justified in the upset I experience when it's time to pay my income taxes.

The ego also encompasses the unconscious, including memories and unresolved issues that are outside your awareness but may still be influencing your thoughts, feelings, and behavior. We have found that there is no need to unearth the contents of the unconscious, as the material stored in this repository is often there for a good reason. In fact, it could be overwhelming to instantly become aware of all this material. As you Awaken, learning opportunities within your Spiritual Curriculum will surface from your unconscious all by themselves in accordance with the Wisdom of your Authentic Self. You can imagine your unconscious as a repository of time-release capsules, each one surfacing in Spirit's timing as a stream of opportunities for your Healing and Awakening.

The most important aspect of an ego's nature is duality. The ego divides all events and experiences into positive/negative, good/bad, and right/wrong, based on the way the ego's belief structure has been conditioned. All experiences pass through your personally constructed perceptual filter and are immediately sorted into a category. As the eminent psychiatrist Dr. David Hawkins put it, "Perception is edited observation."

The ego holds a misidentification with itself as lacking and unworthy. Your perception as filtered through your ego is based on harsh judgments and right/wrong thinking. Ego-centered eyes are not soft eyes that see with Love and Compassion. This is why it's profoundly important to see the Loving Essence within yourself—to look at your Self through the unconditional Loving of Soul-Centered eyes.

The reality of the Authentic Self is Love; it is altogether different from that of the ego. The Authentic Self has no sense of duality. There's no dividing of experiences into right and wrong. At the level of the Authentic Self, you simply see what is. You are fully Awake and Aware of your Essential Nature, which is Love. You'll have experiences that are derivatives of Love, such as Peace, Compassion, Joy, Acceptance, Enthusiasm, Happiness, and (believe it or not) an enhanced sense of Humor.

Recall transcendental moments in your life: a breathtaking sunset over the ocean, looking in your beloved's eyes on your wedding day, seeing your newborn baby for the first time . . . These are examples of times where you saw through Soul-Centered eyes.

The ego allows you to operate in the physical-world reality through the use of your mind and emotions. Through the ego, you can only know about the Authentic Self as a concept or feeling. Since you, like everyone else, were conditioned to be successful in physical-world reality, you've likely come to think of your ego as who you really are. Your efforts may be focused on success in the material world and attempting to get other people to like you so you feel comfortable and experience belonging.

## Moving from Ego-Identification to Authentic Self-Identification

As you Awaken into who you truly are, your ego faces a huge challenge. The presence of a newly discovered Authentic Self, which your ego did not previously know existed, seems to threaten its very existence. In fact, you may even have begun having experiences that transcend the mental and emotional levels that are the domain of the ego. In reaction to this, your ego will often attempt to block efforts at Spiritual development because it views the process of Spiritual Awakening as a threat to its very survival.

Whereas the Authentic Self is concerned with growth, the ego is predominantly concerned with, and attached to, ego patterns such as self-importance, recognition, perfection, glamour, comfort, security, and control, all of which it perceives as essential for survival. Your ego does not realize that maintaining these patterns significantly limits you from experiencing the Peace, Joy, and Fulfillment that are available to you.

However, from a Spiritual perspective, the ego serves a most useful purpose; without it, there would be no arena within which the Healing process could go to completion. Only through the mechanisms of the ego, which operate on the mental and emotional levels, can patterns be stored within your consciousness so that you have the opportunity to heal them.

Understand that your ego has only been serving you to the best of its ability. It should be appreciated and respected, rather than judged for its function. Your ego is a tool best utilized in service to your Authentic Self, which is who you truly are. One of the Principles of Spiritual Psychology says it this way: the mind is a tool to be used in service to the Heart.

When embarking upon the path of Spiritual Awakening, it is simultaneously a major challenge, opportunity, and blessing to move from ego-identification to Authentic Self-identification. It's so easy to fall into the trance of five-sense physical-world reality, looking at yourself and others through the judgmental lens of ego-centered eyes, perceiving through the perceptual filter of good/bad and right/wrong. Your job is to Lovingly educate your ego so that it becomes a willing and faithful servant, one that is dedicated to assisting you in negotiating physical-world reality in service to fulfilling your Spiritual purpose.

It is a game-changing opportunity to see the Loving Essence within Yourself. When you Awaken into the Awareness of the Love that you are, it opens the door to living within the Spiritual Context—that of a Divine Being having a human experience, a Being who simply sees everything as it is and for whom all that it sees is infused with Loving.

Fortunately, Seeing through Soul-Centered eyes is a habit that can be intentionally cultivated to become a Way of Being. The benefit inherent within this approach to life is that it supports you in experientially knowing your Essential Nature as Loving. It is this Awareness that changes everything!

## THIS CHAPTER'S PRACTICES

You've come to an important place in the process of Awakening. Over the years, we have found that it's extremely helpful to have some basic practices that you can rely upon to support your Soul Line focus in a world that appears to want little more than to magnetize you into an exclusively Goal Line way of life. We've designed three such Practices for you here.

The first two are short guided meditations, the purpose of which is to provide you with easy-to-use Practices that move you in consciousness from the Goal Line to the Soul Line. These three Practices alone are sufficient to change your entire life, and we encourage you in setting them up and using them regularly. In fact, the more you use them, the more Aware you will be of living in the Divine Loving of your Essential Nature.

## Meditation for Seeing Yourself through Soul-Centered Eyes

*Take in a deep breath. Slooooow down. That's it . . . and now slooow down even more.*

*Relax . . . and silently set your intention to see your Self through the eyes of your Soul . . . to see your Self through the eyes of Love.*

*Take a moment in the Silence and gently close your eyelids. Focus your Awareness in your Heart, and Inwardly attune to your Loving Essence, which is always present. Simply breathe in Love . . . and breathe out Love . . . Gently follow the rising and the falling of your breath.*

*Experience the Love that is ever present within you, for that is your Essential Nature . . . Remember, your eyes are windows to your Soul . . . and as you experience the Loving within you, we invite you to simply look through the eyes of Love . . .*

*Observe, see, and accept the Beauty and Majesty of your Soul . . . So be it.*

## Meditation on Remembering

*Take in a deep breath and relax. It's time to Remember . . . Time to remember that while you have a body, you are not your body . . . While you have thoughts, you are not your thoughts . . . While you have feelings, you are not your feelings . . . And while you have emotions, you are not your emotions . . .*

*Who are you? You are a Center of pure Loving Awareness . . .*

*Now take in a nice deep breath and let it go . . . And with your next breath, accept that you are a Divine Loving Being living a Divinely inspired life through an Earth School Curriculum designed perfectly to support you in Awakening unto the Majesty of the Love that you are. Breathe this Awareness into every cell in your body for you are, in Essence, Love itself!*

*Be at Peace, be still, and know that you are Love.*

## *Self-Appreciation Practice*

Self-Appreciation is a way of expressing recognition of your worth, value, and Gratitude—for the goodness and greatness of who you are! The following are a few simple examples that I (Mary) currently use. Of course, it's up to you to express your own. Write some down in your journal, if you wish. Focus some of your appreciations on what you do and, more important, Who you are—a Loving Essence, a human being who is truly doing its very best.

- I appreciate that I spent a little time listening Compassionately as our housekeeper shared with me her grief about the sudden death of her sister-in-law in an automobile accident.

- I appreciate that I leave bottled water for our gardener.

- I appreciate the Majesty of my Soul and the nobility and purpose I experience in my work.

- I appreciate my taking time to play with our Darling Isabella (our fluffy cat), sharing sweetness and Loving with her.

- I appreciate my Love of Beauty and the abundant Beauty of the garden I nurture.

- I appreciate the Strength of Heart, Compassion, and Wisdom I bring forward in sharing with others.

- I appreciate my willingness to serve as an instrument of Spirit's Love and Healing Grace.

This simple Practice is a form of Self-Nurturing that adds to the enjoyment and richness of your life. It evokes a sense of Peace, Contentment, and Well-Being. It is yet another way of supporting yourself in a Practice that nurtures Remembering and Awakening into a fuller Awareness of your Essential Nature as Loving.

As I (Mary) was writing this, the doorbell rang. I answered to find our gardener with tears streaming down his face, telling me in Spanish that his mother had died. I immediately called Ron, as my Spanish is rather spotty. The two of us held a Loving space for him as he shared his grief. I'm so grateful for the universal language of Love and Compassion that facilitates communication beyond words.

## INTENTION

I am Seeing the Loving Essence within
myself, experiencing enhanced levels of Self-Acceptance,
Self-Respect, Self-Appreciation, and Self-Compassion,
deepening in my Awareness of my Self as an inherently
Loving and worthy Being—for that is what I am!

# CHAPTER 4

# HEART-CENTERED LISTENING WITHIN YOURSELF

*"Listen and attend with the ear of your heart."*
— St. Benedict

What station are you listening to inside yourself? Is it the jarring judgmental static, the self-critical, restrictive, limiting monologue of what we'll refer to here as station K-EGO? Or is it the nurturing, uplifting tones and tunes of Encouragement, Inspiration, Creativity, Resourcefulness, and Wisdom of station K-L♥VE broadcasting the Unconditional Loving voice of your Authentic Self 24/7?

What's amazing is how simple it is for you to change the inner station. If you find yourself listening inside to the opinionated consciousness of K-EGO sharing its diatribe designed to erode any shred of self-worth within you (not to mention the endless commercials), and you'd like to switch to K-L♥VE, slooow down . . . Take a nice deep breath, close your eyelids, and silently repeat inside yourself: "God bless you . . . I love you . . . Peace, be still . . . God bless you . . . I love you . . . Peace, be still . . ."

In the face of this mantra, repeated slowly and silently within your Heart, the negative voice of K-EGO fades into nothingness, as it can't broadcast at the higher vibrational frequency of K-L♥VE. K-L♥VE is the place where Creativity, Wisdom, Inspiration, Inner Knowing, and Soul Guidance reside—where the answers to your most important questions are available and where your Heartfelt prayers are heard.

Move into your Heart . . . Come into Loving Resonance with your Self. Listen in the Silence . . . Listen to the Still, Small Voice within . . . (And best of all—no commercials!)

### Silence as a Gateway

At first, Heart-Centered Listening may seem like a simplistic Practice. You may wonder why we would even suggest you take valuable time out of your busy life and spend it listening in the Silence. To answer, we turn to the words of the eminent psychologist James Hillman: "Awakening to the original seed of one's soul and hearing it speak may not be easy. How do we recognize its voice; what signals does it give? Before we can address these questions, we need to notice our own deafness, the obstructions that make us hard of hearing . . . For it is hard to get through our hard heads that there can be messages from elsewhere more important to the conduct of our lives than what comes through the Internet, meanings that don't slide in fast, free, and easy . . ."

In our experience, Silence is a gateway to profound Peace. It is also a doorway to your Awakening and the revelation of your Authentic Self. In order to hear the deepest Wisdom of the Spiritual Heart, it is necessary to give yourself time and space for contemplation, reverie, and reflection. When you withhold the gift of Silence from yourself, you are effectively blocking access to the wellspring of Creativity within and the Wisdom, Inspiration, and Guidance of your Soul.

Listening in the Silence while attuning to K-L♥VE invites your Heart and its Spiritual gifts to come forward. It's a key to meditation and experiencing the inner Communion, the Oneness and Divine Love that you are.

And therein lies the value in cultivating this powerful Practice. It's an empowering staple in your repertoire of tools that foster Awakening. Some of the most exquisite experiences arise through Heart-Centered Listening in the Silence. It's basic training for developing your Intuition and Direct Knowing (your sixth and seventh senses). Intuition is often described as a gut feeling and understood to be a person's capacity to obtain or have knowledge and/or immediate insight, without observation or reason. Direct Knowing is receiving a direct transmission of information or guidance from your Soul; it is characterized by the Awareness that you know that you know.

### Outside In—Or Inside Out?

Growing up, most of us were conditioned to think that what happens "out there" is what determines our internal experiences. The mistaken notion is that situations and events happening out in the world are the source or cause of your internal experience. Our goal-oriented world is the consequence of this distorted picture of reality, with everyone engaged in activities designed to make certain that they get their fair share of the pie. This approach is an illusion that seems to make sense in the sleepiness of our human condition, yet it is one of the main reasons there is as much suffering in the world as there is. You could think of it as an "outside in" approach to life.

In this book, we consider an opposite approach—it's your internal reality that draws to you the outer experiences of your life. This notion is expressed in one of the Principles of Spiritual Psychology: "Outer experience is a reflection of inner reality."

Some people may find this proposition outrageous. All we can say is that over the 35 years we've been involved with this work, we've observed thousands of people transform their inner reality and consequently experience their outer world changing for the better.

To ascertain for yourself the validity of what we're saying, we encourage you to turn inward so that you become more aware of your inner experience and your inner life. One way of doing so is to cultivate the Practice of Heart-Centered Listening through inner dialogue. We'll walk you through the Practice step-by-step at the end of this chapter, but first we'd like you to read an example of what this kind of dialogue looks like.

### Attuning to K-L♥VE: An Example of Heart-Centered Listening

When I (Mary) closed my eyes, attuned to the Wisdom and Compassionate Voice of my Authentic Self (K-L♥VE), and asked the questions in the Practice that follows, these answers are what I heard.

Q: What is my life's purpose?

A: *Do not be concerned, Beloved One. Your Heart is open and your path is clear. Continue doing those things you love while paying attention inwardly and outwardly. Continue following the path that has Heart for you as the greater purpose of your life is naturally unfolding. Your Calling, the ways you can serve on the Goal Line of life, have been shown to you from the time you were a child; and you have honored your Calling. Look at the tapestry of your life, and notice the threads of Gold that run through it. Fulfillment comes through sharing your gifts.*

Q: What is my next step in answering and honoring the Calling of my Heart?

A: *Ask Spirit to be shown and guided. Be willing to take small steps (and big courageous steps, too) in the direction of what you experience as having Heart and meaning for you. Notice what doors open to you. Notice too whether what you say you want matches your actions. Work within yourself to bring these into greater congruence.*

Q: How have I been limiting myself or creating a life that's too small for me?

A: *Beloved One, at times you distract yourself with that which has little value for you. And at other times you have allowed the negative messaging of K-EGO to foster self-doubt and feelings of inadequacy inside of you. As you continue your conscious Awakening, you are indeed Waking Up into greater Awareness of the Divine within you, learning how to navigate the High Ground in ways that will support you in residing more consistently within your Authentic Self. Engage in those practices that support you, and you will experience even fuller revelation of the Beauty and Majesty of your Authentic Self—deeper transformation both within your consciousness and in your everyday life.*

Q: How can I experience more of the Love and Joy that are my Essential Nature?

A: *You are learning how to let go of unconscious restrictions, judgments, and misinterpretations of reality—ways of thinking that have blocked you from greater Awareness and experience of the Love and Joy that are your Essential Nature. Rather than identifying with yourself as inadequate and less than, focus on your innate Goodness, your Strength of Heart, and your commitment to Waking Up into the full Awareness of the Love that is your Essential Nature. The deeper Joy and Happiness that you yearn for are within you.*

Q: What are my gifts, and how can I use them in service to myself and others?

A: *Your gifts are your Natural Intelligence, Intuition, Creativity, Humor, Love of Beauty in all forms, and ability to communicate with eloquence and Grace. You are also a natural leader, one in whom others have confidence and trust. You also have hidden talents that you will discover as your life continues to unfold. Stay open to learning new ideas, skills, and ways of Being. You are a conduit for Living Love.*

Remember, you have access to the Wisdom of your Heart 24/7. Station K-L♥VE is always available to you. As our friend Robert Holden says: "Love is listening to your Heart. Ask then, 'What does my Heart want me to know today?'"

## THIS CHAPTER'S PRACTICE

Now that you have a sense of the process, here's an opportunity to ask your important questions and engage in dialogue with your Authentic Self—to attune to K-L♥VE within your consciousness and receive inner guidance as you engage in Heart-Centered Listening within Your Self.

Identify any questions that you have for your Authentic Self and write them down in your journal. Then, following the steps below, listen within and write your answers. If you find that you are not readily accessing any questions at this moment, you may wish to utilize some or all the questions in Step 3.

### *Heart-Centered Listening within Your Self*

Care to conduct an experiment? Follow these simple steps to start an inner dialogue and practice Heart-Centered Listening within Your Self:

Step 1: Silently center your Awareness in your Heart. Remember that Loving is your Essential Nature.

Step 2: Set your intention to open your Heart and attune to station K-L♥VE inside yourself. Give your Self your full attention. Look and listen inwardly with the eyes and ears of your Heart.

Step 3: Silently formulate any question you'd like to ask. We suggest you focus on a question that's meaningful for you at this time. Some sample questions include: What is my life's purpose? What are my next steps in answering and honoring the Calling of my Heart? How have I been limiting myself? How can I experience more of the Love and Joy that are my Essential Nature? What are my gifts and how can I use them in service to myself and others?

Step 4: Now move into the Silence. Open your Heart, attune to K-L♥VE, and ask to receive Guidance in a way you can recognize and understand in accordance with your Highest Good.

Step 5: What do you hear in the Silence? If you don't hear anything in the moment, that's okay. There's no right or wrong way to do this. Sometimes the process of Listening Within to your Authentic Self is a Practice that takes cultivating over time. And sometimes guidance comes as an epiphany when you're in the shower or driving your car.

Step 6: Remember that the Voice of the Authentic Self, the Still, Small Voice within, is always Loving. If you hear judgmental, critical, or negative thoughts, it means you've changed stations and are once again listening to K-EGO. No problem—simply re-center yourself in your Loving and begin again.

Step 7: Perform your own inner "quality assurance" check, referencing your natural knowing and wisdom regarding the integrity and value of the information you receive as it pertains to you. It's always important to check it out!

Step 8: Take a few minutes to write your question and the Awareness you received in your journal. And take a few moments to appreciate yourself for practicing Heart-Centered Listening within Your Self.

---

### INTENTION

I am listening with the ears of my Heart . . .
receptively, Compassionately, with Reverence and Respect.
I am attuning inside myself to K-L♥VE and listening in the
Silence to the Still, Small Voice within.

---

# CHAPTER 5

# SEEING THE LOVING ESSENCE AND HEART-CENTERED LISTENING WITH OTHERS

*"Don't be afraid to look deeply into another person,
for what you will See is truly Beautiful. You will be
aware that what you are Seeing is your Self."*
— RON HULNICK

Do you long for a deeper, more genuine, authentic connection with others? Is there someone with whom you yearn to experience a more intimate Heart-to-Heart, Soul-to-Soul relationship? You can use a variation of two of the skills you just learned, Seeing the Loving Essence and Heart-Centered Listening, to enhance and deepen your relationship with others. These are ways of creating a safe and sacred space within which honest, caring, meaningful communication is much more likely to take place.

When people experience truly being seen and heard, they feel received, understood, and Loved. A space is created within which they naturally open and share those things that matter to them most. This is a deeply affirming experience for both individuals.

People long to be heard. When you are listening, become present in your Heart and give the person before you your full attention. Whether it's your partner, a child, a teenager, a friend, a colleague, or someone you've just met, as you perceive and receive of their Preciousness you'll automatically experience your own.

Consider the value of slowing down and engaging in Seeing the Loving Essence and Heart-Centered Listening with each person you meet. We remember a man sharing with us how practicing these two Soul-Centered skills with his wife had a dramatic life-changing effect. He woke up to the Awareness that he was married to "an Angel." "Further," he said, "I've been an idiot." Their marriage shifted from one characterized by criticism and judgment to a deeply cherishing and honoring long-term Love affair.

While working on this book, I (Mary) realized that my daily life, both personally and professionally, rests on a foundation of Seeing the Loving Essence and Heart-Centered Listening that has become a Way of Being for me. I receive many blessings by simply being with others and listening from my Heart. In our professional work, we facilitate classes, coach clients, and provide mentorship for staff. Our involvement provides continuous opportunities for walking the talk. And as we Awaken, there is a growing congruence in how we conduct ourselves in both the classroom and our personal relationships with others.

It's important here to acknowledge that we're human and still learning. That said, what a Blessing it is to live and participate with others in ways that are authentic, that have Heart and meaning.

### The Healing Power of These Two Skills in Action

Seeing the Loving Essence and Heart-Centered Listening are ways of communicating, "I hear you and I'm here for you. You matter to me." Reflecting on this reminds us of something that happened in one of our early classes.

There were 11 people in the class of our University's very first master's degree program.

At that time, in order to graduate, every student had to demonstrate mastery in effectively utilizing the foundational Principles and Practices of Spiritual Psychology while working with another student. In fact, it was the final requirement for graduation.

On the last afternoon of the last day of the culminating practicum, all but one student had successfully demonstrated competency. This student had one opportunity remaining before he would be required to retake the practicum the following year. And, as if the situation were not sufficiently full of high-stakes elements, we were all aware that his mother was flying in from the East Coast to attend graduation two days later. No pressure here!

The student sat down in his chair to serve as the facilitator. Across from him sat the woman with whom he was to work. As she shared her story, we became aware that what she was saying was very deep and of a nature that could be challenging for anyone to respond to. She went on for some time, and as she went deeper and deeper, I (Mary) found myself thinking, *It's going to take a miracle.*

When she had finally finished talking, she looked at him, awaiting his response. Then, the most amazing thing happened. He went into a deeply Loving place inside himself and slowly, softly, said one simple sentence, "I really hear you, and all I can say is how much I love you."

The woman recoiled as if someone had splashed water in her face. However, she remained stuck—seemingly fixated in the restrictive trance of her tale—and began again, retelling it, adding more details. She seemed totally engrossed in, and identified with, all the specifics of her suffering. When she was done, she again stopped and looked at him, waiting for him to respond.

The student continued to remain centered, residing in a very deep place within. Softly, he said, "I really hear you, and I hear how challenging this is to you—and all I can say is how much, right here and now, I love you."

Once again, the woman pulled back and shook her head as if she had run into a solid object. Within the space of a minute, she began again to tell her story.

And once again, when she was finished, he simply said, "All I can say is how much I love you."

Then it happened. All of a sudden, she broke down and began to sob, tears pouring down her face. From a place of Acceptance and Compassion, he simply encouraged her in expressing all her feelings and crying all her tears. When she was complete, he gently encouraged her into a letting-go process (which you'll be learning later on in this book), which she gracefully moved through and successfully completed.

Needless to say, everyone in the class was ecstatic, and all breathed a huge sigh of relief. Commencement would now be a glorious celebration of the school's first graduating class, with everyone having demonstrated an integration of the foundational Principles and Practices and the ability to effectively utilize them.

When we (Ron and Mary) had a moment to ourselves, we marveled at the Healing Power of Love and how transformational the simplest communication said from the Heart can be: "I hear you, I hear what you're saying, and I care about you."

### A Way of Being

Quintessentially, Seeing the Loving Essence has to do with how you are inside yourself while you're with yourself or another. It's about seeing yourself and others through the eyes of Loving. It is also the essence of the Buddhist greeting *namaste,* which is a conscious recognition that the Soul within me recognizes, acknowledges, respects, and appreciates the Soul within you. It is through this conscious recognition that you realize there is really nothing that needs "fixing" in another Soul. There is only mutual respect, one human being to another. The only language appropriate for two Souls in communication is Heartfelt Loving.

In this sense, Seeing the Loving Essence is not really a skill at all. It's an attitude, a Way of Being. And this attitude, freely shared in combination with Heart-Centered Listening, is the foundation of caring relationships and an important element of all Healing. The presence of these two skills promotes the experience of a safe and sacred space from which Heartfelt caring and honest communication can be shared. The use of these skills encourages two Divine Beings having a human experience to experience the Loving, Healing, and Grace that are naturally present when you open your Heart to yourself and to another, and share the Essence of who you are.

An authentically Loving relationship begins with an Awareness of your already Open Heart. These two skills require that we be present in our Open Hearts and are a continual reminder that residing in the Loving is our commitment and priority. They form the foundation of our marriage and partnership—and after more than 35 years of marriage, we'd say this experiment has been highly successful.

One of the most powerful communications that I (Mary) share with Ron is a Practice we've been doing since before we were married: I open the eyes of my Heart, take him by the hands, look deeply into his eyes, and speaking from my Heart, say, "Darling, I'm here for you. I Love You, I Hear You, and I'm here for You."

## THIS CHAPTER'S PRACTICES

Remember, regardless of what anyone says or does, you can still practice Seeing the Loving Essence and Heart-Centered Listening. In fact, doing so is good for your health, happiness, and well-being. Residing in your Loving Heart also strengthens your relationships and fosters the experience of Awakening.

### *Seeing the Loving Essence and Heart-Centered Listening*

We invite you to practice these steps every day for the next few weeks. We suggest you write your experiences in your journal, for often the experience of simply seeing with the eyes and listening with the ears of your Heart can be quite magical. And, as always, journaling your experiences can positively reinforce and anchor such experiences for yourself.

With another person, follow these simple steps:

Step 1: Center your Awareness in your Heart.

Step 2: Always be aware that you are talking with another Loving Essence, calmly experiencing everything the other person's ego is going through regardless of their current thoughts, feelings, or behaviors. Consciously look for that Loving Essence, for it is always present.

Step 3: Continue focusing your Awareness in your Heart, and consciously attune inwardly to your Loving Essence that is also always present.

Step 4: Keep in mind that the person before you has all the inner resources necessary to effectively respond to their situation.

Step 5: Set your intention to look with the eyes of your Heart and to hear with the ears of your Heart.

### Meditation for Seeing with the Eyes and Listening with the Ears of Your Heart

*Gently close your eyelids . . . and take in a nice deep breath . . . Relax into the Awareness that you are the Presence of Love . . . Experience the Presence of Peace . . . Breathe in the Peace . . . Breathe in the Love . . . Gently follow the rising and the falling of your breath as you relax, cradled in the Loving that is your Essential Nature . . . Now in the Silence of your own Heart . . . slowly repeat the word Love . . . Love . . . Love . . . Continue focusing your Awareness in your Heart . . . and set your intention this day to see with the eyes of your Heart . . . and listen with the ears of your Heart . . . knowing this intention is in harmony with your Essential Nature. Open your Awareness . . . and experience the Beauty of your Loving Essence . . . and the Loving Essence within others . . . the Beauty of the Divine in all things . . . Peace, be still, and know that you are Love . . . Namaste.*

## INTENTION

I am enjoying Heartfelt connection with others
and the Fulfillment I am experiencing, seeing with the eyes
and listening with the ears of my already Open Heart.

# CHAPTER 6

# THE MESSAGE SENT IS NOT ALWAYS THE MESSAGE RECEIVED

*"Three-fourths of the miseries and misunderstandings in the world will disappear if we step into the shoes of our adversaries and understand their standpoint."*

— MAHATMA GANDHI

Albert Einstein's theory of special relativity made an enormous impact on the field of physics when he unveiled it in 1905. It turns out, it is also perfectly valid in the dimension of human relationships—because communication is relative! What you hear from me is a combination of your subjective perceptions of reality as well as mine. For effective communication to take place, we both need to be aware of and respect our individual perceptual differences. It's extremely valuable and freeing to realize that you don't have to agree with someone's point of view in order to come into agreement with that person.

Consider this: each of us is unique. Words in combination with nonverbal expression are our personalized code representing important inner meanings, as well as outer experience. Because we are all unique, effective communication requires we take this uniqueness into consideration. When this is not done, miscommunication sometimes occurs, and the people involved may not even know it. A fundamental error can occur as a result of the assumption that the message sent is the message received.

A perfect example of how the message sent is not always the message received also happens to be one of the funniest sharings we've heard. During a Loyalty to Your Soul Workshop, a public event we offer that is based on the material of our first book, a man recounted how he'd been listening to someone express passionate views about guns. However, the whole time, this man heard the word as *nuns*. He was amazed to hear of their negative impact! You can imagine the laughter that ensued for the two of them and everyone in the Workshop when the misunderstanding came to light.

Unfortunately, this type of miscommunication occurs all too often. You've probably found yourself at the end of more than one conversation, realizing that no "real" communication or exchange has taken place. At times, no doubt, you've experienced the by-product of these fruitless communications—the pain of emotional separation at a deeper level inside yourself and the outer estrangement in relationship that often follows. Sometimes it's as though we might as well have been speaking different languages. Why does this happen?

## The Subjective Nature of Perception

As we've discussed, each of us has a unique internal frame of reference, or perceptual filter, through which we experience life and hear information. It's this perceptual filter that determines what sense we make of events and the information that is presented to us. Oscar Wilde said it this way: "We are all in the gutter, but some of us are looking at the stars."

This calls to mind a wonderful story that appeared on an episode of the classic television show *Touched by an Angel*. In the story, an eight-year-old girl has been acting in somewhat peculiar ways, so her parents take her to a psychiatrist for evaluation.

The good doctor pulls out a Rorschach inkblot test, a psychological test consisting of 10 different pictures on individual cards, composed of inkblot images. The pictures are totally formless, so there are no specific meanings other than what the test taker ascribes to them. As the psychiatrist shows the first card, he asks the little girl, "What do you see?" The little girl responds, "That's a picture of an angel."

To the second card, she responds, "That's another picture of an angel." The third card produces a similar response.

Finally, the doctor says to her, "How is it that you keep seeing pictures of angels?"

The little girl replies, "How is it that you keep showing me pictures of angels?"

Clearly the child's internal frame of reference—her unique perceptual filter—included beliefs and experiences that referenced angels!

### Assumptions, Expectations, Misunderstandings, and Misinterpretations

Your perceptual filter is constructed of beliefs that have been conditioned or "learned." When you observe something, you literally and almost instantaneously process what you've seen through your perceptual filter, leading you to conclude that your interpretation is actually what you've seen. As Dr. David Hawkins said, "Perception is edited observation."

I (Ron) had a marvelous opportunity of observing this phenomenon when, on the occasion of my 50th birthday, we invited my parents to a celebration dinner with some of our close friends. Since I was an only child, my mother loved to tell stories about "little Ronnie" growing up and certainly was not going to allow this opportunity to pass without sharing several. By the end of the evening, I was completely convinced that I have a twin brother somewhere in Creation who shares my name and who had a completely different childhood than the one I remember having. Welcome to the subjective nature of personal reality.

As poet Sondra Anice Barnes wrote:

*The siren blew;*
*The dishwasher*
*Broke down.*
*Now I know*
*That sirens*
*Break dishwashers*

These simple lines are a brilliant example of the associational way in which beliefs are learned early in life, and how convoluted a perceptual filter can become given the misperceptions, distortions, and misunderstandings that so easily and unknowingly get built into it. We then proceed to live our lives as if our perceptions are automatically valid.

It is these embedded beliefs that often result in assumptions and expectations that later on, when not met, can lead to disappointment, frustration, and hurt feelings, which can harden into grievances that often remain unresolved for years.

For this reason, it's worthwhile to do your part to ensure that clear understanding is present each time you communicate with another. One way to do so is through Perception Checking: taking the time to check the accuracy of the information you are receiving at both the content and meaning levels. Reflect back your understanding of what was just said to the other person. Not only does this serve to enhance clarity of communication but it also communicates a powerful relationship message: "You are important to me, and my intention is to do my best to assure that I'm understanding you clearly." This way of being demonstrates your caring and respect, and your intention to understand another, be it your partner, child, colleague, friend, or stranger. You'll find a Practice describing this Soul-Centered skill of Perception Checking at the end of this chapter.

### *When People Feel Heard, They Feel Loved*

Perception Checking is versatile, practical, and powerful. Performed in conjunction with Seeing the Loving Essence and Heart-Centered Listening, it results in clear understanding and greater intimacy in relationships. Remember, when people feel heard (which includes feeling understood), they feel loved.

We both use this skill every day. We consider the foundational Soul-Centered skills of Seeing the Loving Essence, Heart-Centered Listening, and Perception Checking as gateways into a Soul-Centered Way of Being that facilitates all communications—from simply clarifying information such as where to go for dinner to deeper experiences of Heart-to-Heart, Soul-to-Soul communion with a loved one.

By attuning to your Heart, and utilizing these three skills, you'll find yourself naturally hearing another person *and* their meaning. At their sweetest, these experiences become Soul Moments—moments of connection, communion, and completeness. It's been said that the whole is greater than the sum of its parts. These three skills utilized together produce beautiful triptychs of Loving, Caring, and Understanding. You're in the process of building a beautiful palette of Soul-Centered skills, and we encourage you to use them in co-creating your relationships and life.

These three skills are tools of a practical spirituality that brings you into Awareness of the Loving within you. One of the common challenges of modern life for many is the feeling of separation or disconnection and a deep yearning for meaningful Heart-to-Heart, Soul-to-Soul connection. These skills foster the experience of greater oneness with your Essential Nature—with the Loving that you are.

### *Why Perception Is Important in Awakening*

You may be asking whether there are other reasons why the matter of perception is important for someone committed to Awakening. French essayist Marcel Proust summed it up this way:

"Discovery consists not in seeking new lands, but in seeing with new eyes." We invite you to open your Spiritual eyes.

Your openness to new ideas and a willingness to conduct your own experiments using what you are learning in this book, in combination with your intention of Awakening into the greater Awareness of the Love that you are, will in fact provide opportunities for elevating your consciousness and opening the doors of your perception.

William Blake, English poet and painter, went straight to the heart of it when he said, "If the doors of perception were cleansed every thing would appear to man as it is, Infinite. For man has closed himself up, till he sees all things thro' narrow chinks of his cavern." Blake is speaking of the restriction and limitation that occurs when you look through the eyes of your ego. We'll expand more upon this in the next chapter when we explore beliefs and perceptual filters.

I (Mary) have experienced some radical moments in my Awakening in which my perception was altered. As I stepped outside and beyond my ego's field of perception (the "narrow chinks of my cavern"), all at once I was seeing people and experiences through Soul-Centered eyes. Perhaps the best example of this is the shift from seeing myself or someone else through judgmental eyes, then suddenly experiencing my Heart opening, my eyes softening, and seeing with clarity and Compassion. This is why one of my daily prayers has become to simply see and accept what is. It's a way of asking Spirit to assist me in cleansing the lens of my perception and seeing with my Spiritual eyes—Soul-Centered eyes.

## THIS CHAPTER'S PRACTICES

### The Soul-Centered Skill of Perception Checking

The Soul-Centered skill of Perception Checking is a way of slooowing down a conversation and reflecting back your understanding of what you've heard someone communicating. The skill allows you to consciously and respectfully check the degree to which you accurately perceive what has been said up to that point in the conversation.

The good news is that Perception Checking is relatively easy to do once you set a clear Heartfelt intention to learn and practice it. Here's how it works.

When you're in conversation with someone and they are sharing with you, practice Seeing the Loving Essence and Heart-Centered Listening. When the person comes to a natural stopping place, simply say, "I want to be sure I'm understanding what you're sharing with me. What I heard you say is [X] and [Y]. Have I got it?"

If the person affirms that you are in fact hearing them and their message, respond by sharing whatever is present for you that naturally follows. If not, gently ask if they would please share their message again, perhaps using different words, because you really want to hear and understand them.

Every day, strike up at least one conversation with someone in which you consciously utilize the three Soul-Centered skills: Seeing the Loving Essence, Heart-Centered Listening, and Perception Checking. Write about your experiences in your journal.

### *Prayer for Cleansing the Lens of Your Perception*

Consider asking Spirit's assistance in cleansing the lens of your perception through offering a simple prayer. Here is one we like using:

"Father Mother God, I flood my unconscious with purple Light, and I am willing to see, accept, and complete whatever is brought forward. I ask that this be done gently and under Grace, in accordance with my Highest Good. May I see with my Spiritual Eyes—the eyes of my Heart."

## INTENTION

I am slooowing down, coming Present, and engaging in Heart-to-Heart, Soul-to-Soul communications with others, utilizing Seeing the Loving Essence, Heart-Centered Listening, and Perception Checking. My intention is Seeing with Soul-Centered eyes—Seeing and Accepting What Is.

CHAPTER 7

# WHAT YOU BELIEVE DETERMINES YOUR EXPERIENCE

*"If you don't change your beliefs, your life will be like this forever. Is that good news?"*

— W. SOMERSET MAUGHAM

One of the greatest points of leverage available for someone committed to Awakening into higher consciousness is becoming more aware of what you believe. Why? Because, as we shared in the previous chapter, what you believe formulates the lens through which you interpret, or perceive, your experience, which is nothing less than the foundation upon which you have built your life.

And what's so important about that? Only the knowing that when your lens becomes clear or, better yet, nonexistent, your experience becomes one of opening your eyes to What Is, absent of the filtration of interpretation. And when you See What Is, you See that all life is Loving and Beautiful and that your experiential life is filled to the brim with overwhelming feelings—feelings of Awe/Amazement, Gratitude, and Compassion for yourself, life, and for all you See. One of the best descriptions of this experience was written by J. D. Salinger in his short story "Teddy":

"I was six when I saw that everything was God, and my hair stood up, and all that," Teddy said. "It was on a Sunday, I remember. My sister was only a very tiny child then, and she was drinking her milk, and all of a sudden I saw that she was God and the milk was God. I mean, all she was doing was pouring God into God, if you know what I mean."

What Salinger wrote is an exquisitely beautiful account of someone in an Awakened state sharing their experience of Seeing Through Soul-Centered Eyes. It's a lovely reference point of the extraordinary yet everyday, garden-variety mystical experience that's available as you Awaken. The experiences of the many people living in what they experience as restriction, limitation, and lack is just the opposite. Still, it takes courage to open your eyes with the intention of recognizing and dismantling your perceptual filter of limiting beliefs, misinterpretations of reality, and misidentifications that are restricting your Awareness and coloring your experiences.

For now, consider the possibility that your current reality is being perpetuated in large part by beliefs you hold. Let's take a closer look as to why that might be so.

## Prisms of Perception and Discovering Your Rainforest Interpretations

It is well known and accepted in the study of psychology that what you think and believe about everything, including the nature of reality itself, constitutes the perceptual filter through which you see the world. And further, your beliefs are actually the building blocks through which you are creating your life. What you believe is usually based upon the way you interpreted what you heard and experienced growing up, as well as the inner decisions and outer decisions you subsequently made regarding how you live your life.

An example of this is found in a wonderful book, *The Forest People* by Colin Turnbull, in which he writes about his experience living with the Mbuti Pygmies in the rainforest of the Belgian Congo. A group of scientists went there to study the Pygmy culture in the rainforest where the Pygmies lived and where visual references are largely vertical.

One day, Colin drove with his young Pygmy guide, Kenge, to the open plains of a national park. Motioning to several buffalo a few miles away, the guide asked what type of insects they were, then laughed at Colin's insistence that they were indeed large animals. Colin then describes Kenge's reaction to driving closer to the buffalo herd:

> He watched them getting larger and larger, and though he was as courageous as any Pygmy, he moved over and sat close to me and muttered that it was witchcraft. Finally when he realized that they were real buffalo he was no longer afraid, but what puzzled him still was why they had been so small, and whether they really had been small and had suddenly grown larger, or whether it had been some kind of trickery.

While the Pygmy people were aware of open, horizontally referenced areas outside of their home, they had developed a largely vertical frame of reference from living in the rainforest and did not have the same *perceptual references* as those who grew up in open spaces.

With this story in mind, each of us might entertain the questions: "What rainforest interpretations am I making up of which I'm unaware?" and "What stories have I been telling myself that just might not be true?"

You construct your perceptual filter and perpetuate your personal mythology through internalizing beliefs based upon your family patterns, cultural values, environmental influences, and religious training—your basic rainforest upbringing. These often result in limiting beliefs, misinterpretations of reality, erroneous conclusions, and misidentification with a story of self-victimization, self-sabotage, and unworthiness.

Let's see how this dynamic operates in everyday life in areas such as relationships, finances, and health. Since money is a big issue for many people these days, we chose the following example as it illustrates how your beliefs affect not only your financial kingdom on the Goal Line, but also your internal process of Awakening on the Soul Line.

## Dismantling a Perceptual Filter:
## Getting Free of Money Myths

Recently, I (Mary) had a lovely conversation with a very accomplished and successful businesswoman regarding some financial challenges. This highly educated professional was experiencing a cycle in which clients were getting excited about projects, committing, and then unexpectedly putting them on hold. It had occurred with 10 significant projects over the last three months, and it was creating financial difficulties for her personally as well as for her business. She was highly motivated to discover if something in her consciousness might be contributing to this pattern, because while she and her business partner had occasionally experienced this over the years, it had never been to this degree.

Together we began an exploration based on two Spiritual Psychology Principles: "Outer experience is a reflection of inner reality" and "Personal internal reality is subjective. Therefore, what you believe determines your experience."

She had grown up in affluence, living in a beautiful home on a large property complete with a live-in gardener and cook. Her parents had been generous with her in many ways, including completely paying for an Ivy League education and studies abroad. However, the messaging and conditioning she received from her parents and grandparents was such that she experienced a lot of "nos" when it came to items she'd *like* to have: "No, you don't need that," "No, maybe later," "No, it's not necessary. . . ." Thus, her internal conclusion became "I can't have what I want," especially when it came to big items like international trips, luxury clothing, or designer handbags. She developed an internalized pattern of restrictive beliefs when it came to her personal wants and items that could be considered luxuries.

As a consequence of being repeatedly told "no," she had many experiences throughout her childhood and adolescence of frustration, disappointment, and anger—however, these emotions were "stuffed" in service to being a "good girl." As a student of Spiritual Psychology, she was aware that these feelings needed to be acknowledged, expressed, and released in service to freeing herself from this story that was now playing out with her clients and, to some degree, continuing to play out with her parents.

I gave the businesswoman the following "home assignment" based on the first step of a Practice at the end of this chapter.

### Uncovering Limiting Beliefs

Briefly and honestly describe at least five limiting messages you received about money as you were growing up. In exploring this, consider the following:

- What and by whom were you taught?

- Was there consistency between what your parents taught you and the way they were/are with money?

- What were the "rules" you learned about money/ wealth and what you can or can't have? (Write the limiting messages down as a list.)

Her responses to this final question were:

- "We are not rich and we have to be careful about how we spend our money."

- "We can't buy what we want."

- "You can't have what you want that is unnecessary; you can do with less."

- "It's a virtue to spend as little money as possible, especially when it comes to luxury items."

- "If you want something, you can't have it now. You have to wait until later."

- "We can't spend money the way your friends can. We can't buy you the things that they buy. It's not necessary."

- "It's important to live below your means so you don't run out of money."

After thoroughly completing the process, she reported, "It was very clarifying. The belief that has the most charge and has created the most contraction and obstacles is this: *If I spend too much money on what I want, what makes me happy and brings me joy, I will be punished by not having any money for the necessities of life."*

She recognized that as long as she continued holding to the truth of this matrix of beliefs and operating from inside this perceptual filter, she was limiting her ability to achieve the financial results she desired and to which she aspired. Her clients' behavior of postponing projects indefinitely was mirroring her internal belief structure—the interpretations she had made of her experiences growing up.

### Liberation from the Deeper Underlying Misinterpretation

As the woman and I continued our conversation, it was evident that embedded within this limiting belief was a deeper belief: that the acquisition of things and/or experiences *out there,* those things that money can buy, is what makes you happy and brings you joy. As you can see, this is purely Goal Line, ego-referenced thinking, in contrast to the deep inner knowing at the Authentic Self level that you are already Happy, Joyful, Loving, and Abundant—in fact Complete, Whole, and Enough. In other words, there was a deeper misinterpretation inside that was promoting a consciousness of lack.

This is a great example of how the ego perpetuates its story of unworthiness—that you are not enough—and the opportunity for liberation from that story. A little later in the book, we'll be introducing the most powerful tool we know for letting go of these kinds of beliefs and misidentifications.

When you begin to catch on that, rather than an ego caught in a field of illusion, you are actually a Divine Being having a human experience, the game changes. You can choose to no longer be seduced by the messages of limitation and lack found within the false self, characterized by "I'm right; you're wrong," "I'm upset because . . . " "I can't do that," "I can't have what I want," and "I'm not enough."

Now you can recognize that these positions only perpetuate judgments, limiting beliefs, and misidentifications of yourself as separate and unworthy. You realize you can make choices that release the ties that bind you to these limiting beliefs and Awaken experientially into your Authentic Self.

The most expansive context we are aware of has to do with Waking Up. And the biggest Wake Up is waking up *experientially* to the reality of your inherent Loving nature—that you are a Divine Being having a human experience.

### It's an Inkblot World

The courageous woman whose story we shared is a beautiful example of the value of examining your perceptual filter and identifying the matrix of limiting beliefs that are creating challenges for you. These challenges are, in reality, amazing opportunities. They are all part of your Divinely orchestrated Earth School Curriculum, which is tailor-made to support you in Awakening into your Loving Essence.

By understanding that you interpret outer experiences through the perceptual filter of your internal belief system, you recognize that we live in an "inkblot world." With this Awareness, you can learn to work with the metaphorical feedback that your experience reveals to you about your perceptual filter and the beliefs you hold in consciousness. And you can learn the liberating process of letting go of restrictive beliefs and choosing others that can better serve you now.

Most people are completely unaware of the underlying perceptions that are at the root of their emotional reactions. It is for this reason that anytime you feel upset about anything, an empowering question to ask yourself is, "What is the underlying belief beneath the emotion or feeling I am experiencing?" Answering this question is a huge step, one that is essential to freeing yourself from the unnecessary mental and emotional suffering that so many people experience.

And do you know, at least in our experience, what single belief (or should we say *misbelief*) results in far more psychological disturbance than any other? Believing, for whatever reason, that you are unworthy or unlovable—anything less than a Divine Loving Being who is having a largely ego-centered human experience.

The more you Awaken, the more you'll experience your inherent, hardwired worth and value, which is independent of anything you think, say, or do.

## Freedom

Imagine living inside a house with no windows. The only view of outside is through a tiny keyhole in the door.

And now imagine that you receive a key that allows you to unlock the door and venture outside to experience blue skies, glorious sunshine, and a 360-degree vista displaying the beauty of nature. Imagine the Joy, Freedom, and Aliveness you would feel being released from the prison of your limited keyhole perception.

Know that Awakening into your Authentic Self is very much like that. After all, isn't it time you came out from your rainforest?

## THIS CHAPTER'S PRACTICE

### Freeing Yourself from Limiting Interpretations

If you find what we've shared intriguing, then this Practice is tailor-made for you. This Soul-Centered skill is one of the most powerful ways we have experienced of identifying some of your limiting beliefs, which are the barriers you maintain against the Awareness of your Essential Loving Nature.

Utilizing the process as outlined below, we invite you to seek and dissolve at least one of the barriers within you that stand in the way of your living your life in greater Freedom, Peace, Loving,

Joy, Wisdom, Creativity, Beauty, and Enthusiasm. As it has for many others before you, it could just change your life!

Choose a situation—any situation—that you'd like to transform and that surfaces negative thoughts and feelings when you think about it (for example, a relationship, your finances, the state of your health, or your career). Write about the situation in your journal and then consider the following questions:

1. What are your thoughts about this situation and how do you feel about it? Allow yourself to be vulnerable about it. Be honest with yourself and as specific as possible.

2. Within the context of this situation, are there any specific beliefs you have about yourself that relate to any of the following statements?

- At times, I judge myself as unlovable, unworthy of the good things of life, not capable, shameful, or deserving to be punished.

- Sometimes I feel as though I'm not enough, that nothing I will ever do will be enough or good enough.

- I often feel that it's important for me to prove my own worthiness through my achievements.

3. From the Wisdom of your already Open Heart, is there another belief you *could* choose to hold that you suspect would result in a more positive feeling? What would that belief be?

4. If you were to choose to adopt this new belief, what do you anticipate would be the result?

Write your answers to these questions in your journal. You may find that the more times you engage yourself in this process, the freer you will feel emotionally.

## INTENTION

I am freeing myself from any limiting beliefs that shackle me to the misidentification of myself as unlovable or unworthy. I am replacing them with positive, Self-Affirming beliefs in service to living in greater Joy and Freedom as I am Awakening into the Awareness of my Essential Loving Nature.

# CHAPTER 8

# BECOMING A
# SPIRITUAL SCIENTIST

*"Do not be too timid and squeamish. . . All life is an experiment.*
*The more experiments you make, the better."*
— RALPH WALDO EMERSON

Everyone appreciates the benefits that science provides. Even the Dalai Lama speaks of its value—and with good reason. The results of scientific inquiry speak for themselves. The scientific movement began in earnest at the time of the Industrial Revolution around 1760 and has been going strong ever since. It has largely become the way of the world precisely because it is so well suited for producing results in physical-world reality. No one doubts the amazing advances in the quality of life that have been made—or the destructive potential that has emerged as well.

For our purposes, we are not discussing the pros and cons of what has resulted in physical-world reality from scientific methodology. Rather, what we are interested in is the scientific method itself, for within that method there exists tremendous opportunity for accelerating Spiritual Awakening.

As Emerson said, "All life is an experiment. The more experiments you make, the better." Why might Emerson have said this? Perhaps he was aware, as we are, that many people simply do not like the thought of changing due to the ego's attachment to familiarity—as manifested in the ego patterns of security, comfort, and control. However, people love to run experiments. Interesting, isn't it?

### The Four Steps of the Scientific Method

So what's an experiment and how do you engage in one? Basically, there are four essential steps involved in the process.

Step 1: You pose a question you are seeking to answer.

Step 2: You set up a tracking system that accomplishes two experimental objectives:

- *Measuring of results.* This involves the developing of a "unit of measurement" that will provide you with a starting point (where you are when you begin the experiment) and a finishing point (where you are when you complete the experiment.) It is this difference between what you measured before you began and what you measured after you completed the experiment that you will base your conclusion upon.

- *Assuring your participation.* This involves a calendar so you can track the number of days you actually participate in your experiment, including the steps you take on each day, so that you have a clear record of what you've done.

Step 3: You design an experiential process, the carrying out of which will provide you with data regarding the question you've posed.

Step 4: When you have completed the experiential process, based upon your measurement of results, you evaluate your data, reach your conclusion, and determine what, if any, further experiments on this subject you wish to conduct.

This four-step process is designed to work extremely well in physical reality. You can readily see how well such methods function by thinking about scientific advances such as the automobile and television, and current realities like space stations and a man walking on the moon, to say nothing of the Internet and cell phones. And this doesn't even begin to consider developing technologies such as 3-D printing, the mining of asteroids, nanotechnology, and genetic engineering.

## Accelerate Spiritual Awakening Using the Scientific Method

Less known, but equally valid, is the use of the very same scientific method for purposes of Spiritual research and Awakening. The only real difference is that in the physical sciences, results are public, measureable, and easy for all to see. Advancements in physical science are easily understood and readily replicated.

In Spiritual Reality, results tend to be more personal, internal, and subjective. And this condition will continue until such time as sufficient people Awaken more fully into the sixth sense of Intuition and the seventh sense of Direct Knowing, at which time the validity of subjective personal internal experiences will become more universally known, knowable, and accepted.

Now here's the really cool part! Whether you realize it or not, when you develop an experiment based in Spiritual Reality, the very act of engaging in it causes you to place yourself in the consciousness of what we call the *Spiritual Scientist*. In other words, you are functioning in exactly the same way as a scientist does in physical-world reality—only you are not looking for results "out there" in the physical world. You are conducting research within the domain of your own personal internal experience within your consciousness.

In other words, rather than looking to see how something external has shifted, you are developing a method designed to perceive changes that are occurring inside of you. It's based in terms of your own personal experience, which is a completely different perspective from what we're used to. (Although you may discover that the inner results of your experiments do in fact have an effect in your physical-world reality.)

We're happy to say, however, that if our highly experiential classes are in any way indicative, more and more people are designing and participating in such experiments and discussing their results with others reporting similar experiences. It's exciting and a real mind-blower! It validates the statement we're hearing more and more these days: the last major frontier is consciousness.

## Say Hello to Your Neutral Observer

Now that you've had an introduction to the Spiritual Scientist aspect of your consciousness, you're ready for the next step—and it's a big one. It has to do with *how* your Spiritual Scientist conducts experiments: the attitude of Neutral Observation.

What do we mean by *Neutral Observation*? Let's suppose that you enter into an experiment with a bias, holding fast to preconceived notions about how the experiment *should* go. If it doesn't go that way, you may very well come away disappointed and frustrated, perceiving that it wasn't a very good experiment. However, if you enter the experiment with no particular expectations, you're free to *neutrally observe and experience* the results of the experiment based upon nothing but the *what-is-ness* of the outcome.

A wonderful example of what we're referring to appears in the book *Stranger in a Strange Land* by Robert A. Heinlein. There is a character by the name of Anne, who is referred to as a Fair Witness. In order to demonstrate to someone what this means, the teacher, pointing to a house on a hill, asks, "Anne, what color is that house?" Anne looks to the house and replies, "It's white on this side." Anne would never assume what colors the rest of the house was painted because she could not see them at that moment. *Fair Witness* would be an excellent synonym for the ways the Neutral Observer perceives the world.

### Learning Neutral Observation from a Rat

I (Ron) had my first exposure to the power of Neutral Observation during my freshman year at college. As a psychology major, one of my first classes was Experimental Psychology. The course was all about learning how we learn, and it included a lab during which we studied rats in mazes and how they learned to run them. The lab consisted of only 12 students, so we had ample opportunity to ask questions.

During the very first lab, the professor entered the room carrying a small cage with a white rat. The cage was set up in such a way that the rat had access to a lever. Small pieces of food would automatically be delivered through a small passage to the rat whenever it pressed the lever.

The professor said nothing while he set up the apparatus. He held up some small pieces of food and simply said, "This rat has not been fed for three days." That was it.

We all watched to see what would happen. Every now and then, as the rat scampered about the cage, it would inadvertently press on the lever. As pellets of food dropped into the cage, the rat would promptly devour them, then continue its exploration. It didn't take very long until the rat was standing beside the bar, repeatedly pushing the lever to obtain as much food as it wanted.

Then the professor said, "For your homework assignment, write a short paper describing what you observed."

Perceiving myself a good student, I wrote something to the effect that the hungry rat learned to press the lever to get some food. When my paper was returned to me, words like *hungry* and *learned* were highlighted and next to them was written, "You did not observe this."

In our next class, those of us who had received the same feedback questioned the professor as to what he meant. He said, "You did not observe *hungry*, nor did you observe *learned*. What you observed was an increase in the amount of lever pressing of a rat that had not been fed for three days as a result of following each lever press with a pellet of food. That's what you actually observed."

When you are functioning from within the consciousness of the Neutral Observer, you report only what you can *actually observe* in any given moment. You assume nothing. Observing free of an agenda is one of the most powerful abilities you can develop in service to the process of your Awakening, because this is what it means to See from the perspective or altitude of your Authentic Self. You have no opinions, interpretations, or desires pertaining to what you are observing. This is a very different way of being in the world compared with your ego's dualistic right/ wrong approach of interpreting everything you see!

## A Growing Experiment

I (Ron) engaged in what I perceived to be a rather radical experiment many years ago. I was having a dental challenge such that I was experiencing bone loss in one area of my mouth. X-rays showed exactly where the loss was occurring, so I decided to run an experiment with the intention of regrowing bone in that area—something generally thought impossible without medical intervention. My strategy was to research the process of how bone grows, cell by cell, and see if I could affect the process through a specific Spiritual exercise. I was fortunate in that my dentist said that he knew of someone who had accomplished this success-fully—and if he could do it, why not me?

After I perceived I understood the process, every time I brushed my teeth, I would visualize new bone cells growing in the two relatively large "pockets" that had been forming as the bone deteriorated around certain teeth. There was no way I could tell how I was doing during the process, as my only point of compari-son would be pre- and post-visualization X-rays. However, every morning and evening, I was faithful in my practice. Finally, after about a year, I went in for a new set of X-rays, and sure enough, sufficient bone had regrown to replace much of that which had deteriorated. The pockets had filled in to the point that they were no longer considered a concern. My dentist loved it!

My major learning from this experiment was not so much that I was capable of growing bone in my mouth—something that I would have thought impossible—but that *my consciousness has a great deal more authority and power in my life than I had previously imagined.*

And here's a really important key for shifting patterns both in physical reality as well as Spiritual Reality. When you design your own experimental process, set it up so that you are doing small steps consistently. That way, every time you complete a step, your consciousness will register a sense of successful completion, thereby positively reinforcing that step and setting you up for the next one. As we like to say, "Small steps taken in strategic places often result in significant outcomes."

An example for us is writing this book. Which do you think would turn out to be a more effective, fun-to-do, positively reinforcing approach: Celebrating with a party only after the final words have been written? Or committing to writing for a minimum of three hours a day for at least four days each week, thereby honoring our commitment, and celebrating each completed chapter? The second, right? Why? Because each day we succeed, we have the inner satisfaction of acknowledging ourselves for honoring our commitment. And, at the end, by all means, let's still have the party—a really nice one with lots of friends.

The good news is that your Spiritual Scientist loves to run experiments and evaluate the results. So let's see if we can set up an experiment so that you can experience how you can utilize this method in service to your Awakening. Incidentally, you can use this method anywhere in your life to enhance results in whatever area you choose.

### Fully Utilize Your Spiritual Scientist

Choose an area of your experience you would like to explore more fully utilizing your inner Spiritual Scientist. Relationship experiments are popular. Here, we use the example of wanting to enhance your relationship with your spouse, partner, parent, child, colleague or friend, or another person in your life. For this experiment, it's best to choose someone you'll see or talk with every day, or almost every day.

#### Setting Up Your Experiment

Step 1: Pose your experimental question. For the purposes of this experiment, we'll use the question: "What, if any, will be the results in my relationship with this person by engaging in certain specific attitudes and behaviors with them over a period of two weeks?" (For example, Seeing the Loving Essence, Heart-Centered Listening, and Perception Checking will probably work really well.)

Step 2: Set up a tracking system that accomplishes two experimental objectives:

- *Measuring of results.* Measuring quality of relationship is not the same as measuring something physical like weight loss for which there is a handy little device known as a scale. For this, we need an internally referenced scale. Okay—let's develop one.

  At the end of this chapter, you'll find a nine-point Overall Quality of Relationship scale that a USM student developed several years ago. It worked very well for him, and several others have also used it with good results. Feel free to use it for this experiment or come up with your own. In Appendix B, you'll find the process for designing your own rating scale, as well as three examples.

- *Assuring your participation.* This involves using a calendar so that you can track the number of days in your experiment, including the steps taken each of those days, so that you have a clear record of what you have actually done. This involves simply taking a calendar and marking it accordingly. For example, let's say that you commit to conducting your experiment for 14 days, beginning on June 2 and ending on June 15. On your calendar, you mark "1" in the box of June 2, "2" in the box of June 3, etc.

Step 3: Design an *experiential* process, the carrying out of which will provide you with data or evidence regarding the question you've posed. For this experiment, you might choose the process of having a conversation every day with a particular person, during which you'll practice the Soul-Centered skills of Seeing the Loving Essence, Heart-Centered Listening, and Perception Checking.

Step 4: Carry out the experiential process. Then, based upon your measurements, evaluate your results, reach your conclusion, and determine any further experiments on this subject you might wish to explore.

### Ready, Set, Go!

Here's how you would carry out the suggested two-week experiment in this Practice:

**Day 0:** The day before you begin your experiential process, take the temperature of your relationship with your chosen person. Review the nine-point Overall Quality of Relationship scale at the end of this chapter, and honestly choose the rating that best fits the current state of your relationship. Write that number down in this date's box on your calendar.

**Days 1–14:** For these 14 days, you'll be carrying out your experiment. Engage in conversation with this person while utilizing the Soul-Centered skills of Seeing the Loving Essence, Heart-Centered Listening, and Perception Checking. Be sure to do this Practice daily, or as often as possible. Mark your calendar to keep track of the days, and be sure to journal about each of your conversations. This record will anchor your experiences and provide you with learning that may be useful in future relations.

**Day 15:** The day after you have completed your experiment, again review the Overall Quality of Relationship scale. Select the rating that now best describes the current state of your relationship with that person and compare it with the rating you chose before you began the experiment.

There are only three possibilities: the new rating will be greater, lesser, or pretty much the same as the old rating. In any case, you have now likely learned a great deal about yourself and your relationship with this person. As you evaluate the results of your experiment, take special note of what you have learned, rather than focusing on the particular number of the rating. We strongly suggest you write about it in your journal.

## INTENTION

I am a Spiritual Scientist conducting my own personal research, practicing the attitude of Neutral Observation.

## OVERALL QUALITY OF RELATIONSHIP:
### Daily Rating Scale

*Intention for this scale:* I choose the rating that best describes my perception of the current state of my relationship with [Name] as I experience it inside of me.

1. Either very negative communication or none at all
   Very strong judgments
   Strong feelings of upset, anger, and/or guilt
   No experience of caring or appreciation

2. Communication is very difficult
   Strong judgments
   Frequent feelings of annoyance, frustration, and/or hurt
   No experience of caring or appreciation

3. Very little real communication
   Judgments present although less intense
   Feelings of annoyance, frustration, hurt
   No experience of caring or appreciation

4. Some communication
   Judgments still present although continuing to soften
   Feelings of annoyance, frustration, hurt
   No experience of caring or appreciation

5. Some communication
   More aware of choice between Acceptance and judgment
   Feelings of upset are less intense
   Open to possibility of expressions of caring or appreciation

6. Some communication at a more honest level
   Acceptance more frequent than judgments
   Feelings more pleasant
   Open to possibility of expressions of caring or appreciation

7. Communication is more free and clear
   More Acceptance of our differences
   Still occasional upset but generally positive feelings
   Some experience of appreciation

8. Communication is very free, honest, and sincere
   Acceptance is now the predominant mode
   Feelings of warmth and Compassion
   Genuine expression of Caring and appreciation

9. Communication is magical, Healing, and Heartfelt
   Unconditional Acceptance
   Strong feelings of Loving and Compassion
   Deep appreciation and Loving expression

# CHAPTER 9

# ACCEPTANCE: A GATEWAY TO FREEDOM

*"If you would only switch on the light of awareness and observe yourself and everything around you throughout the day, if you would see yourself reflected in the mirror of awareness the way you see your face reflected in a looking glass, that is, accurately, clearly, exactly as it is without the slightest distortion or addition, and if you observed this reflection without any judgment or condemnation, you would experience all sorts of marvelous changes coming about in you . . . It is this nonjudgmental awareness alone that heals and changes and makes one grow."*

— ANTHONY DE MELLO

How did you do with your experiment in the previous chapter? Most important, what did you learn? Over the years, we've found that our most valuable gains didn't emerge from the results of our experiments—as amazing as some of those results were!—but through developing the Spiritual Scientist's approach to life.

When I (Ron) first heard about this approach of the Spiritual Scientist, I questioned it. At first, I couldn't see why this was being given so much emphasis. And then, slowly, I began to catch on. The greatest value wasn't in the fact that it made me a more keen observer (though it did), nor that it made me see life more clearly (which it also did), but rather in the state of Awareness I had to enter in order to become the Neutral Observer and See through its eyes. I had to become a Fair Witness. And it is this switch in my way of Seeing that changed, and continues to change, everything.

## A Whirling Windmill—What to Do?

Some years ago, we were in Santa Fe, New Mexico, for a few days of rest and relaxation. It was a gloriously sunny winter day with the kind of clear blue skies one finds only in the mountains of New Mexico. We were chatting and leisurely strolling, arm in arm, down one of Santa Fe's charming narrow downtown streets on our way to one of our favorite shops. Suddenly, as we approached an intersection, we noticed a man off on a diagonal to our right. Though he was across the narrow street, he was rapidly moving directly toward us, and his arms were whirling like windmills.

I (Mary) found myself letting go of Ron's arm and moving away from what seemed like an inevitable encounter with the fellow. My fight-or-flight mechanism had kicked in and, heart pounding, I scurried away! It was clear to me the man was experiencing a deep disturbance within his consciousness and was to be avoided.

Ron, on the other hand, simply stopped in his tracks. As I watched, heart in my throat, Ron became completely quiet, standing in Stillness. And when the man came face-to-face with Ron, all Ron said in a voice of Peace and tranquility was, "Please don't." Ron serenely stood in the Presence of Peace, giving the fellow nothing to resist or hook into.

As I watched in amazement, the man turned and whirled away from us. I rushed to Ron's side, overflowing with Gratitude that nothing had happened, yet knowing that something miraculous had occurred. All Ron could say to me was, "I don't know what I did. I really don't know what happened. I just 'let go' and went into a place of total Acceptance. I was looking down and didn't even see where he went."

What Ron experienced, and what anyone engaging in Neutral Observation will experience, has been referred to as the first Law of Spirit: Acceptance. Learning to See this way is described in the lovely quote by Anthony de Mello at the start of this chapter. To simply observe "without any judgment or condemnation."

Sounds pretty easy, doesn't it?

While it is relatively easy to understand, by now it's probably becoming more clear that understanding something is not the same thing as having mastery of it. You may understand how a bow and arrow work, but it is quite another thing to consistently shoot an arrow into the bull's-eye! In this way, as in most areas of life, it takes a great deal of practice and experience to turn "understanding" into "mastery." The process of Awakening, for most people, is no different. Michelangelo put it this way: "If people knew how hard I have had to work to gain my mastery, it wouldn't seem so wonderful."

Now here's the good news. Acceptance is a gateway to Freedom. Believe it or not, you really do have the power to choose to move through this gateway by simply observing and *neutrally* acknowledging what is. It's the "neutrally" part that is most challenging for most people. So let's start by broadening our understanding of what Acceptance is and what it means to live more fully in the consciousness of the Neutral Observer.

### Five Types of Acceptance

In our work over the years, we've observed five general areas where people appear to have the greatest challenge moving into Acceptance. To begin, we'll share our definition of *Acceptance*, which is "truly being okay with what is." It means *observing neutrally* that the house is blue on this side—and residing inside myself in the place where that's okay with me. You know that you're in Acceptance when what you observe is okay with you—meaning you have no argument with the house being blue—on this side.

1. *Acceptance of What Is:* Accepting what you observe with *neutrality* rather than having any emotional charge, good or bad, about it. If you have a charge

about it, you are not in Acceptance. Now perhaps you can see why we say this is easier said than done.

2. *Acceptance of Self:* Accepting all of you—your humanity, as experienced largely through your personality or ego, as well as your Divinity, which is experienced when you are Awake within your Authentic Self.

3. *Acceptance of Others:* This means Accepting everyone based on your understanding that we are all, literally, in this life together and that everyone is, in Spiritual Reality, a Divine Being having a human experience. Really, as hard as it might be to believe, we're all doing our best given our conditioning, experience, and level of Awareness.

4. *Acceptance of the World Just as It Is:* Accepting everything that is presently happening on this beautiful planet as well as everything that has ever happened here. For many of us, this is a really tough one.

5. *Acceptance of God:* Accepting the possibility that there is more going on in our lives than what we observe in physical-world reality. It means Accepting the possibility that there is purpose behind it all, regardless of whether we perceive or believe it.

As we said previously, it is no easy thing to move into Acceptance within any one of these areas—much less all five of them. That, however, is the direction in which we are headed.

### *The Benefits and Possibilities of Acceptance*

Assuming you move into greater levels of Acceptance, what then? How does that affect how you tend to show up in the world? Let's consider some of the possibilities that are revealed when we consciously choose Acceptance.

## The Freedom to Choose Your Attitude

Some people have expressed to us the concern that, as they advance in the direction of Acceptance, they will become like doormats and have no real say in what goes on around them. Actually, nothing could be further from the truth.

To ease this worry, we'd like to share one of the best examples pertaining to this perceived dynamic from Viktor Frankl. He was an Austrian psychiatrist imprisoned in a concentration camp during World War II, and wrote an epic book called *Man's Search for Meaning* after his release. Among many other things, he shared stories of kindness among the suffering, such as the men who selflessly gave away their last piece of bread to fellow inmates. He didn't judge the guards as different from the prisoners, but looked on all with Compassion. He operated not as a "doormat" but from a place within when he wrote: "Everything can be taken from a man but one thing: the last of the human freedoms—to choose one's attitude in any given set of circumstances, to choose one's own way."

## Disagreeing without Being Disagreeable

Another misconception that has been expressed to us comes from people who believe that if someone disagrees with them, they must "take up arms and do battle" to prove the rightness of their perspective. These people often experience emotional distress, a sure sign that Acceptance is not present. Often, their learning consists in experiencing the possibility that we can disagree without having to be *disagreeable* with each other.

There's something beautiful about having the quality of relationship with someone where you can say, "You know what? I have a different perspective on this than you do. Perhaps we can discuss our reasons for what we believe to be best, and maybe even both learn from each other." When you can enter into this level of conversation, it is a sure indicator that you are Awakening.

### Distinguishing Resignation from Acceptance

Perhaps the most common misunderstanding is the distinction between Acceptance and Resignation. Acceptance is *truly being okay with what is.* Resignation, on the other hand, is *saying* you're okay with what is for externally based reasons, but not really being okay with what is.

Sometimes in resignation, there is an attitude of defeatism—an expectation of loss or defeat. And of course, what makes this sort of dynamic additionally challenging is that sometimes the person who is in a state of resignation is simply biding their time until they can change whatever it is they have not Accepted. That's not a formula for Happiness or success.

## Acceptance Doesn't Mean You Like or Agree with What Is

When you move into Acceptance, it tends to affect how you show up within yourself, especially when facing challenging situations. Believe it or not, there's tremendous leverage in Accepting something, although you may not be in agreement with it. And why is that? Because you'll experience yourself as centered, calm, clear, and in balance, rather than disturbed and upset. Your inner experience will be that of cooperating with what is, and then calmly deciding what your response will be and what action you'll take—without ever experiencing yourself as upset or disturbed. You'll be recognized and appreciated for your equanimity even in difficult situations.

### "He Tried to Stab Me!"

I (Ron) was once called in to consult with the director of a small facility for adolescents who had run afoul of the law but were too young to be placed in prison. When I arrived, the director took me on a tour of the facility grounds, then we went back into the main building to meet some of the staff and residents. As we were getting settled, there was a tremendous disturbance out in the yard.

Suddenly the door burst open and in came a staff member in obvious disturbance. She was sobbing deeply and kept repeating, "He tried to stab me. He tried to stab me."

She was almost immediately followed by two of the male staff. They were grasping the arms of a 12- or 13-year-old boy so that he could not move away from them. The director looked at me, held out his arm in a gesture of invitation and said, "Dr. Hulnick?"

The first thing I noticed was that as terrified as the woman looked, the boy appeared to be even more so. I could immediately see from his face and demeanor that his life had not been a very happy one so far.

I turned to the woman and asked what had happened. Apparently there had been some sort of miscommunication, and she moved toward the boy, whereupon he pulled out a knife and threatened her. I asked her how she felt when he pulled out the knife. She said how frightened she had become and how surprised she was because she really liked him and thought they were friends.

At this point, the young boy began to sob. He said how scared he was because he didn't understand what was happening and because he thought she was his friend. As you might imagine, it quickly de-escalated from there and didn't take long for the tension to melt. In hindsight, it turned out to be a truly beautiful learning experience for everyone involved.

When it was all said and done, the director turned to me and said, "How did you do that?" I assured him that I was as surprised as he was at how it turned out. Perhaps the most important thing was that I Accepted the boy and didn't judge what he had done. I Accepted *him* and his behavior, even while not agreeing with his behavior.

Remember, Acceptance doesn't mean you have to *like* what is. And it doesn't mean you have to *agree* with what is. And it certainly doesn't mean you can't put effort into *changing* what is. It simply means that you're not *at war* with what is, you're not *fighting* with what is, and you're not *judging* what is. Rather, you simply Accept what is and then decide how you'll choose to respond.

It's important to realize that your liking or disliking something has absolutely no effect whatsoever upon that something. But it sure has a lot to do with what's going on inside of you—your state of consciousness in that moment—for when you are in Acceptance, you are in a state of Peace.

## Accepting Your Humanness: Loving Your Self No Matter What

To reside in Self-Acceptance is a radically different way to be in a world predisposed to blame, wrong-making, and "I'm upset because . . ."

To Accept or to judge yourself, that is the question! Why? Because, whether you're aware of it or not, it's your very own ego that is serving up a menu of thoughts and feelings that are recipes for a *lot* of mental anguish and emotional suffering. Your feelings are thoughts felt physiologically, so the domino effect can be an avalanche of painful inner experiences including guilt . . . shame . . . embarrassment . . . humiliation . . . hurt . . . grief . . . disappointment . . . despair . . . and unworthiness, to name a few. These feelings often snowball, leading to a sense of deep separation from your Authentic Self; the automatic by-product of this is unhappiness. It's a cold and icy inner terrain when you're caught in what can seem like a blinding blizzard of negative thoughts and painful emotions.

The Beautiful Blessing in all this is that the hearth of your Heart is ever warm with the Light of Living Love. And . . . your Loving is the antidote! It is an antifreeze and snow-melting compound rolled into one. Opening your Heart and bringing forward the warmth of Self-Compassion and Self-Acceptance for your humanness will thaw and dissolve even the most resistant of judgments and negative beliefs.

By embracing the Spiritual Psychology Principle "All of life is for learning," your unresolved issues simply represent your limiting beliefs, judgmental thoughts, negative self-talk, and upset feelings, which become opportunities to embrace your humanness, to Accept your thoughts and feelings—and, bottom line, to Love yourself no matter what.

I (Mary) remember a challenging time that I experienced more than 20 years ago having to do with Accepting my own humanness. My nights were characterized by periods of wakefulness in which I experienced very painful feelings of separation and unworthiness. For a long period of time, I would wake up in the night feeling miserable and very aware of my deep suffering. I would attempt to shift my focus and energy by calling up inner images that were comforting to me. (My Beloved Pie Face, a little cat I had as a child, was a favorite.)

Eventually, I realized that I needed to more strongly take dominion in my consciousness. I began to flood my consciousness with Loving and chanted a mantra as a way of redirecting my focus: "I Love myself no matter what . . . I Love myself no matter what . . ."

Within a few days, I had a powerful dream that represented a complete shift in consciousness and revealed to me that I was Beloved by Spirit. The negative pattern lifted and has never returned.

Your humanness and your human experience are to be Accepted, appreciated, and cherished for what they truly are. Being in human form is the most exquisite opportunity for Awakening. Your human experience, your unique Earth School Curriculum, is a Spiritual Blessing especially selected, chosen, and carefully packaged by your Soul for you.

Receive it in Loving with Strength of Heart and remember: your thoughts, feelings, beliefs, judgments, reactivity, and upsets are signals letting you know where to direct the Breath of Acceptance, Loving Compassion, and Forgiveness. They are not who you are. Identifying with them only deepens the freeze. Loving brings the balmy breezes of Acceptance, Compassion, Loving-Kindness, and Healing Grace. Rest assured, the transformational thaw is underway.

We encourage you in flooding all levels of your Consciousness and every cell in your body with the Light of Living Love. I checked with K-L♥VE this morning; it's 72°F and sunny in the

Authentic Self. You're learning how to apply empowering tools through which you can regulate your inner thermostat.

We'll get into them in more depth in upcoming chapters. For now, suffice it to say that inside the Spiritual Context, the everyday things that disturb your Peace represent unresolved issues. When you address them with Acceptance and Compassion, they present opportunities for Healing and become rungs on the ladder of your Spiritual Awakening.

## THIS CHAPTER'S PRACTICES

In this chapter, we offer two options designed to support you in moving from the negative state of reactivity and judgment into Acceptance. Notice as you engage in these processes how your emotional reactivity neutralizes, your mind clears, and you experience the inner Peace, Calm, and Freedom that come with Acceptance.

### *Moving into Acceptance*

Here's a three-step process through which you'll have the opportunity for experiencing what moving into Acceptance is like. You can repeat the steps as often as necessary.

Step 1: Identify one situation that is your version of a "whirling windmill": something that appears to be coming toward you and about which you have concern. How do you feel? Write about your experience and feelings in your journal.

Step 2: Now visualize yourself moving into Acceptance. Take a deep breath and simply move into Accepting the situation as it is. Remember, Acceptance has nothing to do with your likes or dislikes or whether you agree or disagree. Simply Accept what is. After all—what you are experiencing has nothing to do with your Essential Nature.

Step 3: Now how do you feel? Did you experience any change? Write about your experience now and the experience of shifting into Acceptance.

### I Accept Myself No Matter What

We encourage you to conduct a personal experiment regarding Acceptance. (Refer to the four-step process in the previous chapter.) Ask Spirit to flood your consciousness with Loving and chant the mantra, "I Accept myself no matter what . . . I Accept myself no matter what . . ." at intervals throughout the day. In fact, this is a great Practice to do looking in your own eyes in the mirror. Write about your experiences in your journal.

---

**INTENTION**

I am Accepting my life and all its situations
and circumstances as they are. I am Accepting What Is,
my Self, Others, the World, all that goes on here, and God.
And I am Loving and Accepting myself no matter what.

---

# CHAPTER 10

# TO ACCEPT
# OR TO JUDGE:
# THAT IS THE QUESTION

*"For there is nothing either good or bad, but thinking makes it so."*
— WILLIAM SHAKESPEARE

In the previous chapter, we explored the dimension of Acceptance and the process of Neutral Observation, which is your way of Seeing when you reside in the state of Acceptance. In this state, which we refer to as the consciousness of the Authentic Self, all experiences are perceived through the lens of Loving and seen *neutrally* for what they are.

You may be saying to yourself, "This all sounds easy enough. Okay, I get it. From now on I'll simply choose to see everything neutrally from the perspective of my Authentic Self. Is there more I need to know?" In fact, there's a lot more you'll discover as you Awaken.

You may recognize that you are a Soul having taken human form, one that is experiencing life in physical-world reality. However, when you look out through the perceptual filter of your consciousness, what you see is instantaneously followed by your interpretation intended to make sense of what you've perceived. It's in this process of "making sense" out of what you perceive that you have a choice, and there are really only two possibilities: seeing through ego-centered eyes, a process of judging—or Seeing Through Soul-Centered Eyes, a process of Accepting. Let's first take a look at the ego's perspective, with its automatic by-products of mental anguish and emotional suffering due to the ego's inherently judgmental operating system.

## Seeing through Ego-Centered Eyes

Judgment is the process that creates the internal experience of separation and abandonment that then leads to feelings of shame, guilt, and the inner misidentification of your self as unlovable and unworthy. Let's see what this looks like by diagramming the process as follows:

### JUDGING (Seeing Through Ego-Centered Eyes)

| Perceptual Filter (Prejudiced) | | Emotional Reaction | Action |
|---|---|---|---|
| R I G H T | G O O D | I am HAPPY Because . . . | Judging Leading to Actions/Choices that are Biased, Restricted, and Unclear |
| W R O N G | B A D | I am UPSET Because . . . | |

Things Happen } What Is }

Here's how it works. You begin with an Awareness that "Things Happen." And whatever is "Happening" is "What Is" at that moment in time. As a Self-Aware being, you observe "What Is," and your mind, utilizing its perceptual filter of conditioned beliefs, almost immediately sorts the data into one of two possible categories based upon your beliefs and values.

This sorting process occurs almost instantly as an instinctual act of self-preservation. Humans have evolved in this way because at one time our very lives may have depended upon it. After all, if you're about to be attacked by a man-eating animal, you don't want to be spending much time thinking about whether or not it's a good idea to get out of reach as quickly as possible!

In today's world, you can clearly see that the attitude of judging—making someone or something good/bad, right/wrong—is epidemic on the planet at this time. Relationally, this challenge is reflected in the unprecedented level of divorce and family estrangement. Nationally, judgment and wrong-making are at the root of all dissension and war. As the Dalai Lama said: "We can never obtain peace in the outer world until we make peace with ourselves."

Since we all come with egos as part of our standard human operating system, we all have opportunities for learning to deal with our judgments and the emotional reactivity of "I'm upset because . . ." It's an inner choice to enter into a right/wrong interpretation of anything. No matter how strongly you believe that your point of view is the "right one," taking that position leads automatically to negative emotional reactions such as hurt, anger, and disappointment. If you believe that something is "right," you'll tend to feel "good" about it. And if you believe it's "wrong," you'll tend to feel upset and disturbed about it.

Said another way, anytime you enter into judging, you will experience a negative emotional charge—you'll feel disturbed or upset. Unfortunately, these reactions tend to get anchored in the body, and this results in habitual emotional response patterns to certain situations. Once a habit forms, we tend to lose track of the underlying interpretation upon which the negative emotional reaction is actually based. This leads to a kind of knee-jerk reactivity that characterizes moments of opinionated conscious-ness and chronic "I'm upset because . . ."

"Good grief," we hear you saying, "I wasn't aware of that. Can we please talk some more about the other possibility you men-tioned earlier?"

Of course. The other possibility is Acceptance and it looks like this.

## The Choice to See through Soul-Centered Eyes

**Seeing Through Soul-Centered Eyes—ACCEPTING**

| | | Perceptual Filter (None) | Authentic Self Response | Action |
|---|---|---|---|---|
| Things Happen } | What Is } | Objectivity, Neutral Observation | Loving, Acceptance, Compassion, Peace, Equanimity | Objective Evaluating Leading to Actions/Choices that are Neutral, Balanced, and Clear |

Acceptance is challenging for most people, as it's not the way we've been conditioned as we grew up. Rather, we were taught, as was so accurately portrayed in the musical *South Pacific* many years ago, "to hate all the people our relatives hate." And if you look around the world today, humanity is still struggling to learn another way. And that new way begins with Acceptance.

When you're residing in a state of Acceptance, you are in a Loving state of Peace, one that is free of the right/wrong biases of the conditioned beliefs that comprise a perceptual filter. Within that state, you are free to enter into the process of *evaluation* rather than judgment, righteousness, and condemnation. You evaluate, which simply means you look for the value without the overlay of right and wrong. This is also known as Neutral Observation, the approach of the Spiritual Scientist. You may not like what you see and you may not agree with it—yet you remain neutral about what is. Your Peace is not disturbed.

While you may not have consciously thought about it previously, evaluation is something you do every day. For example, when you go to a restaurant, you evaluate and simply choose what you'd like—let's say the grilled cheese sandwich. What you don't do is get upset with all the other sandwiches and salads on the menu, and demand that the restaurant discontinue serving them because they're bad foods. (Well . . . maybe some of us do that.) Can you see that evaluation is simply a process of whether you choose to see things as they are or choose to see them through the perceptual filter of your ego's conditioned beliefs?

The good news is that your decision of whether to observe neutrally or through a right/wrong bias happens in your mind. As we've learned over the years, the mental realm is the easiest to work within as it's the only level in consciousness over which you have full dominion. What we're saying is that you really do have the ability to reinterpret earlier experience and thereby redefine your reality. When you let go of limiting beliefs and the misidentification of yourself as unworthy, your mental, emotional, and behavioral choices change accordingly.

The key lies in surfacing those underlying limiting interpretations that have become beliefs. Then you can release them and choose new perspectives that better serve you now. After all, life presents a myriad of opportunities for learning to let go of judgment and choose Acceptance. Everyday situations might include: the dry cleaner couldn't get the stain out of my new dress, the chef put too much dressing on my salad, my boyfriend broke up with me, my stylist cut my hair too short, the housekeeper broke one of my mother's antique crystal goblets. Advanced experiences might include: my child was hurt in a fight at school, my partner received a challenging health diagnosis, I discovered my teenager is using drugs, I unexpectedly lost my job, one of my parents died suddenly . . . And on it goes.

## Inmates Learn Freedom to Choose

A real-life example of the power of Acceptance comes from our Prison Service Project, a project that we have been involved with at the University of Santa Monica. It all started around 15 years ago when we received a letter from an inmate at Valley State Prison for Women in Chowchilla, California. The woman inquired as to whether we might be interested in sending someone up to give a talk to inmates to assist them in boosting their self-esteem.

I (Ron) didn't know what we could offer or whom we might send, but the letter itself was very Heartfelt, so I kept placing it at the bottom of my correspondence folder and allowing it to make its way to the top in the hopes that a satisfactory answer might appear—which it eventually did.

At that time, USM was offering a program in Soul-Centered Leadership that included a service opportunity selected by each student. I thought that one or more of the students might like to be of service through visiting the prison and talking with the inmates. At last I had a way to respond to the prisoner who had originally written to me. She replied immediately and put me in touch with the woman who was the Director of Education at the prison.

To my surprise, I learned that through some miscommunication, the director thought we were agreeing to send several women to lead a workshop for the inmates. I quickly realized that Spirit was at work here to reveal an infinitely better plan than the one I had envisioned. Truly, a Soul-Centered workshop focusing on skills of Healing and transformation could be a much more powerful way of serving the women of this prison. So we agreed to send a group of 20 USM graduate volunteers.

Fast-forward—the first workshop was a tremendous success! Forty hardened "lifers" became vulnerable, opening their hearts to themselves and each other. They let go of guilt, shame, and deep levels of remorse and self-judgment. The program quickly grew in popularity with the inmates. It evolved to the point that twice a year, some 70-plus USM grad volunteers were traveling to Chowchilla at their own expense to participate in a two-day workshop with 150 to 250 inmates, sharing with them the Principles and Practices of Spiritual Psychology. In recent years, the program has grown even further, evolving into the creation of a charity, the Freedom to Choose Foundation, that serves multiple prisons annually. (If you'd like to watch a heart-warming video and learn more about it, enter "USM Service Project: Freedom to Choose (Part 1)" in an Internet search engine and enjoy the ride.)

And do you know what the inmates continually reported as the most powerful and helpful skill they learned from the USM grad volunteers? That's right—Acceptance!

It turned out that in this particular prison—and I suspect this is common within many incarcerated populations—fights erupted fairly frequently among inmates, and whenever they did, the women in proximity experienced pressure to pick a side. In so doing, they often got physically involved, the net result being that all perceived to be fighting were "written up." These reports were entered in the inmates' records and counted against them at the time they became eligible for parole.

Enter the Soul-Centered skill of Acceptance. Here's how it was practiced in the prison workshop: One inmate shared something of her choice to another inmate, following the guideline that it be something about which she felt strongly. No matter what she shared, the only response the other inmate could say is, "I hear you, and I hear what you're saying." Or, as we learned to say in prison, "I'm pickin' up what you're puttin' down."

No one had ever told these women that they didn't have to pick a side in a fight—that they could simply Accept that a fight was occurring and they could choose to respond neutrally. Their attitude could be one of, "I hear you both, and I'm not picking a side." The USM grad volunteers reported that, time and time again, the inmates shared that this one skill was the most valuable.

Now here's something for your consideration. Can you imagine how liberating it would be if more of us living in the restrictions of our self-imposed prisons learned to practice that attitude and skill?

> ╱ **THIS CHAPTER'S PRACTICE** ╲

### *Choosing to See and Accept What Is*

Are you ready to conduct an experiment consisting of shifting from ego-referenced perception to Authentic Self perception and experiencing what can happen? The following five-step experiment will help you experience what we mean by choosing to See Through Soul-Centered Eyes.

Run through it right now to get the feel of it. Then, we recommend you experiment with using it with situations that may occur in your daily life. You can write your responses to these questions in your journal.

Step 1: Briefly describe a recent situation that triggered a negative emotional reaction inside of you. What happened? How did you feel? What did you do?

Step 2: Assuming the premise that underlying every feeling is a mental perception or belief, what were your perceptions or beliefs associated with this situation?

*Clues:* What "should" they have done differently? What was "wrong" in this situation? What would be "right" according to your beliefs?

Step 3: From the Wisdom of your Authentic Self, is there another perspective or belief you could choose to hold that you anticipate would result in a more positive feeling or sense of greater equanimity? If so, what is it?

Step 4: If you were to choose to hold this new perception, how do you anticipate you'd feel?

Step 5: By choosing it, how do you perceive your experience may be different the next time you find yourself in that situation?

## INTENTION

I am Seeing Through Soul-Centered Eyes—Seeing and Accepting What Is—experiencing greater Peace, Equanimity, Clarity, and Loving in my everyday life.

CHAPTER 11

# REFRAMING ISSUES AS BLESSINGS

*"The gem cannot be polished without friction,*
*nor man perfected without trials."*

— Confucius

In the last chapter, you were introduced to an in-depth portrayal of the processes of judgment and Acceptance. Hopefully, you saw how easy Acceptance is to understand, and yet how challenging it can be to practice. Believe it or not, this is not a bad thing.

You may be asking, "How so? My experience with judgment has been less than glorious. In fact, it's contributed to a lot of anguish and suffering." We hear you! The good news is that this Awareness allows you entrance into a game-changing arena that can be affirming in your intention to Awaken more fully.

Let's say, for example, that you experience relative Peace and equanimity around 25 percent of the time—you're somewhat Awake. About 75 percent of the time, you're in some level of disturbance—pretty "sleepy" at the time. Where would you think the opportunity is for you to Awaken? It's in the 75 percent!

The way you can easily identify the 75 percent is to look at where you experience disturbance, for the simple reason that wherever you have disturbance, you will find that you have judgment. And wherever you have judgment present, you have the opportunity of releasing the judgment, thereby moving into Acceptance.

In Spiritual Psychology, we refer to the art of utilizing the Principles and Practices in service to your Awakening as Working Your Process. Engaging in this process requires that you summon the willingness, courage, and self-honesty to explore the situations and circumstances that trigger disturbance inside of you—and more specifically, to explore the mental and emotional material that has surfaced when you find yourself becoming upset—no matter how justifiable your upset seems.

We define these experiences of disturbance as *unresolved issues*. While they are generally experienced emotionally, they are based upon judgments you are making that have their roots in particular beliefs and definitions of reality you hold to be true (your perceptual filter). Can you see how this all ties together?

We like to present this information as the Anatomy of Beliefs:

- Emotional reactions are physiological responses to thoughts and perceptions.

- Thoughts and perceptions are subjective and a function of beliefs.

- Beliefs are composed of interpretations of early experience learned in accordance with Spiritual Curriculum.

- What you believe determines your experience, including your emotions.

## The Spiritual Context and Spiritual Curriculum

It is for this reason that we developed a Soul-Centered skill named Reframing Issues as Blessings that can only be truly understood and appreciated when considered from inside the Spiritual Context. In fact, there are a cluster of Spiritual Psychology Principles that set the stage for understanding the value of your Spiritual

Curriculum and how it relates to this particular skill. Here are seven of them:

- We are not human beings with Souls; we are Souls using a human experience for the purpose of Awakening.

- Earth functions as a school for Spiritual Awakening and everyone registers for their specific Curriculum.

- Your Spiritual Curriculum consists of unresolved issues as well as opportunities for service, sharing your gifts, and living into your Heartfelt dreams.

- An unresolved issue is anything that disturbs your Peace.

- Unresolved issues are not bad; they're simply part of your Spiritual Curriculum.

- Unresolved issues are blessings, as they are opportunities for Healing and Awakening.

- How you relate to an issue is the issue; or, how you relate with yourself as you go through an issue is the issue.

There's no argument that life is filled with challenges. Some of them are relatively minor and some are huge. Examples of rather large challenges include illness, the death of a loved one, a financial reversal, loss of position, family crisis, shifts in business, and natural disasters. Each one of such situations can catalyze feelings of disorientation, upset, discomfort, fear, grief, or anger—all very understandable responses to a perceived loss of control and disruption of what's familiar to you.

There are also the seemingly less significant challenges. Examples of these include someone cutting you off in traffic, inconsiderate behavior on the part of a family member, a child not complying with your request, the perception that you are not being heard, or being treated unfairly at work. Like situations deemed major, these events or circumstances can also trigger feelings of upset, anger, hurt, discomfort, fear, and other negative emotions. You get the idea.

What's essential is not the magnitude of a challenge, but rather the quality of your response to it—how you are with yourself within your consciousness as you navigate your way through the challenge. The first step is honestly assessing whether you are reacting to a particular challenge with Acceptance or with judgment.

## The Opportunity within Spiritual Bypass

And herein lies a potential stumbling block. Your very own ego will sometimes attempt what we call a "spiritual bypass." What this means is that you will tell yourself and others that you are in Acceptance about something—*saying* "it's really okay"—but in actuality, you are not in Acceptance, and inside of you "it's not okay." What can make this even trickier is that you usually don't even know you're doing it.

How does Spiritual bypass occur? Generally, it's fostered by a reluctance or unwillingness to be truly vulnerable—a hesitancy to experience the uncomfortable emotions associated with a past or present event. In our experience, this often occurs because at an earlier time in your life, you didn't have the Awareness or support necessary to assist you in processing through to resolution the uncomfortable thoughts and feelings triggered by the challenging experience. Therefore, it's likely your way of coping with the feelings was to stuff them down and tell yourself platitudes in an effort to comfort yourself and alleviate the emotional pain. You construct a story of okay-ness—a Spiritual bypass—as a way of protecting yourself from feeling the disturbing feelings.

Obviously, when you bypass something, it doesn't go away. So if you attempt to bypass emotional pain, you are actually placing yourself in an unhealthy situation, psychologically speaking. Eventually, the pain will find a way to emerge, as your own Soul knows that the only way the pain can be healed is by bringing it forward and letting it go. This is the reason why unexpressed emotional pains tend to fester and worsen over time, often contributing to health challenges.

In terms of the Spiritual Curriculum, unresolved issues are opportunities. And if you don't address them here and now, the same or similar situations will disturb your Peace at a later time. Thus there is infinite opportunity for Healing and Awakening. And here's some really good news: you have an amazing amount of inner support that will reveal itself to you as you muster the courage and dare to engage in this level of inner work.

You're probably beginning to see that there's actually Wisdom in choosing to do this courageous inner work. As written in *A Course in Miracles*, "Your task is not to seek for love, but merely to seek and find all the barriers within yourself you've built against it." We add to that, "And to dissolve them."

## Unresolved Issues Are Not Bad, They're Opportunities for Awakening

Usually, judgments can be found in the same general areas as Acceptance:

- Type #1: Acceptance of What Is vs. Judgment of What Is

- Type #2: Acceptance of Self vs. Judgment of Self

- Type #3: Acceptance of Others vs. Judgment of Others

- Type #4: Acceptance of the World as It Is vs. Judgment of the World as It Is

- Type #5: Acceptance of God vs. Judgment of God

Once again, it's essential to bear in mind that the single best indicator of whether you are in Acceptance or judgment is whether something disturbs your Peace. If something upsets you, you are in the land of judgment—and this is not a bad thing. Being disturbed doesn't make you "wrong" or a "bad person"; all it means is that in this particular area, you've just uncovered another opportunity for Awakening.

Now comes the most important part of this chapter—the Awareness that makes it so much easier to seize the opportunities present when you move into mental and/or emotional disturbance. Rather than seeking to *avoid* your disturbance, *acknowledge* it as soon as possible. Why? Because you recognize that unresolved issues are not bad; they're simply part of your Spiritual Curriculum. As such they are blessings that reveal opportunities for Healing and Awakening.

When you engage in this process, you are recognizing and acknowledging your inner disturbance as feedback from Spirit that "school is in session" and you are, in fact, free to use your disturbing experience in service to your Awakening. In short, you'll be engaging in the empowering process of Reframing Issues as Blessings.

Think this might be powerful? Here's a letter we received from a USM grad that is a breathtaking example of someone making extraordinary use of the process of Reframing Issues as Blessings and the results she experienced.

> *Dear Ron and Mary,*
>
> *Please excuse me for not using the proper stationery—I don't have any at hand and want to take this opportunity, these free moments, to share with you. I am enclosing a check. It is part of the tithe on my inheritance from my two sons who died last October. I decided to share it with all the people and institutions who have touched and shaped me, and helped me realize who I am.*
>
> *My deepest thanks to both of you for the experiences you invited me into through the two-year Master's Program in Spiritual Psychology.*
>
> *When my two sons died by suicide last year, it was only because I've learned to look at life as a learning opportunity that I was able to stay in one piece. Thanks to the teachings of Spiritual Psychology, I was able to choose to see their deaths as*

*a sacrifice in order to send a message to our Family. This atti-
tude has resulted in forgiveness between their father and myself
and in deepening of relationships between their siblings.*

*I know I am a more deeply feeling and loving person because
of my sons' deaths. I live my life remembering (and demonstrating) what they wouldn't . . . that life is beautiful and satisfying.*

*Thank you so much for preparing me to be able to respond
in this way.*

Emerson was aware of this dynamic when he wrote, "Bad
times have a scientific value. They are occasions a good learner
would not miss." He clearly saw that unresolved issues represent a
golden opportunity to bring forward the Strength of your Heart as
this woman's words so beautifully express. In the face of her two
sons' suicides, she chose to look through the eyes of Love and to
see all life as beautiful, sacred, and satisfying.

It is these very experiences, challenging as they may be, that
when properly understood and utilized can provide some of the
greatest opportunities for learning—grist for the mill of your
Awakening. As the saying goes, we can complain because rose
bushes have thorns or rejoice because thorn bushes have roses.

Thus, life's everyday challenges (and the emotional upset they
trigger) become opportunities for utilizing the Soul-Centered skill
of Reframing Issues as Blessings. As soon as you shift your perspective from the reactive, issue-driven approach to life of "I'm
upset because . . ." to a Soul-Centered Learning Orientation to
Life, you're opening a door to Freedom. Your attitude automatically shifts from upset, judgment, powerlessness, and resistance to
one of Acceptance, Compassion, Creativity, and Resourcefulness.
Initiative and Authentic Empowerment naturally follow.

Here are two key questions you can ask yourself to assist you
moving into higher consciousness when you're upset: "What new
learning is in store for me now? What golden opportunity do I
now have for Awakening into the Love that I am?"

Remember, how you relate to the issue *is* the issue. Or, said
another way, how you relate to your Self while you go through the
issue *is* the issue. Healing and Awakening begin here.

## Becoming the Blessing

One of the most inspirational people we have known is a woman by the name of Betsy Taylor. When we met her more than 30 years ago, she was a white-haired woman with five grown children, one of whom had epilepsy and another who had Down Syndrome. If those were not challenges enough, some years before we met her, she had been hit by a car and endured a long, painful hospitalization and rehabilitation. Her body was filled with metal plates and screws, and she followed a daily regimen of a few hours of exercise in order to maintain her mobility.

However, these events and circumstances were not the Betsy Taylor story. The Betsy Taylor story was a story of someone residing in Unconditional Loving who truly saw and experienced everything as a Blessing—an opportunity for Love. She was a massage therapist whose reputation was par excellence, bringing Blessings of Divine Loving and Healing to both the body and consciousness of whomever she touched.

As the years passed, Betsy became more challenged physically. After her hip replacement surgery, she restored her ability to walk through clear intention, a discipline of physical rehabilitation, and daily exercise. Later, her diabetic condition worsened, and one of her legs needed to be amputated above the knee. Though challenged, she was undaunted in her intention to serve with Love— to be the Presence of Love.

In all the time we knew Betsy, she was impeccable when it came to the Spiritual ecology of her consciousness. She knew, as Thomas Jefferson purportedly said, "The price of liberty is eternal vigilance." When disturbance surfaced in her consciousness, she was all over it! She did the necessary work to restore her inner environment to one of Peace and Loving.

Betsy loved to volunteer at USM during class weekends. She considered it a privilege to sit in the classroom. She often told us that part of it was selfish on her part, as when she was present in the energy field of the class, she was pain free. On the other hand, we considered it a great Blessing that Betsy chose to be of service at USM, as she was a true battery of Spiritual Light and Loving. The other volunteers loved her dearly and would seek her out and bask in the Presence of Love that emanated from her, drinking in her words of Wisdom and Loving Kindness.

About two years before she passed over, Betsy moved to a retirement center two blocks from the University. She would drive her bright-red motorized cart, crossing busy Wilshire Boulevard in Santa Monica, to assume her self-appointed post as Light Bearer. What a Spiritual Warrior!

To us, Betsy actually transcended the Skill of Reframing Issues as Blessings. She did this through Being the Presence of Love, the Blessing incarnate. Here are a few lines that she wrote about two weeks before she made her transition.

*I believe in the magic of life,*
*This magic has been showered upon me.*
*I continually live in Grace and in that belief;*
*Life has been beautiful,*
*Even to the Gracious Beauty of death.*
*I am truly lucky and feel so bountiful,*
*And in this bounty*
*I am continually devoted to Spirit*
*And in that support and in that Love,*
*I am honored by the Grace and revelation of God.*
*I am breathless!*

Betsy's story is one of the alchemy of Awakening, the transmutation of the ego's challenges into the Pure Gold of the Authentic Self.

The French word for "wound," *blessure,* has the same root as "blessing." In this we find evidence of the Divine Perfection— and thus the Skill of Reframing Issues as Blessings. The very things that "wound" you are, in fact, the vehicles that when properly utilized become rungs on the ladder of your Spiritual Awakening, assisting you in realizing your Essential Nature—Divine Love.

> ## THIS CHAPTER'S PRACTICE

### *Reframing Issues as Blessings*

Identify a minimum of three challenging situations that trigger a disturbing or upsetting emotion for you. Write about the situations and what disturbance each is triggering for you in your journal.

For each situation, ask yourself the following two questions and write your responses in your journal:

- What learning opportunity might this situation be presenting to me now?

- What golden opportunity do I now have for Awakening more fully into the Awareness of the Loving Being that I am?

Then, practice Reframing the Issue as a Blessing. Notice and journal any shifts in your Awareness and energy that you experience as a result of engaging in this process.

## INTENTION

I am strengthening my spiritual muscles by looking for the Blessing in challenging situations in service to releasing a judgmental, issue-drive orientation to life and experiencing the ascending energy of the Presence of Love within me.

CHAPTER 12

# TRANSCENDING YOUR COMFORT ZONE

*"Verily the lust for comfort murders the passion of the soul,*
*and then walks grinning in the funeral."*

— KAHLIL GIBRAN

Congratulations! You've already covered a great deal of ground. By this time, you're likely moving forward with some momentum, and you may be encountering a certain degree of resistance or inner opposition from your ego to your intentions to Awaken—and to participating in the practices conducive to Awakening. This is completely normal. In fact, everyone who chooses to consciously participate in Awakening will, sooner or later, face their first major obstacle—the fear of the unknown. Let's consider this dynamic, the way it operates, and how to successfully move through it.

Think about it. The very fact of Awakening means that you are daring to venture outside of your comfort zone into the unknown. What you Awaken *into* is largely unknown to you experientially, although you may have read about it and talked with others who claim to have had the experience. For many people, this can be a frightening prospect. After all, the comfort zone is comfortable for the very reason that it is *familiar.*

We are creatures of habit. Based on our past experiences, the interpretations we've made, the conclusions we drew, the perspectives we hold, and the learning we've gleaned, we've erected certain beliefs that define our comfort zones and tend to navigate our lives accordingly. Can you see that this is clearly an ego-centered approach to life?

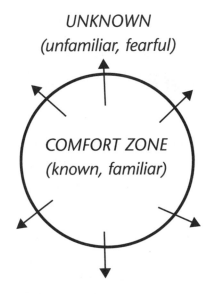

*UNKNOWN*
*(unfamiliar, fearful)*

*COMFORT ZONE*
*(known, familiar)*

The Ego's Perspective

### *The Ego Patterns*

To maintain its comfort zone, the ego utilizes three major patterns—comfort, security, and control—all designed to maintain your life the way that it is. Let's consider each of them.

### Comfort

The ego pattern of *comfort* involves your seeking to make choices that support familiarity. Your ideal picture of life has already been erected, and some part of you doesn't want it to change. "I've got my pictures, and I want to keep them as they are."

The range of comfort is vast. For some people, living on the edge or repeatedly taking big risks is what they find comfortable. Another person could find continual change to be comfortable, perhaps using it as a way of avoiding commitment based on a fear of being trapped. Or consider this one: hiding your Light under a bushel and living a *small* life as a way of avoiding visibility and taking responsibility for sharing your gifts. And so on.

## Security

The ego pattern of *security* is characterized by engaging in behavior that provides a sense of safety. "If things are consistent and reliable, then I can feel okay (safe, secure). And if they aren't, then I feel betrayed or abandoned."

## Control

*Control* is often referred to as the "master addiction," and it is also based on the ego's search for safety and security. Control is the ego's effort to hold things in place—to maintain the status quo, where it believes it knows how to win at the game of life. It can be used to maintain comfort, achieve security, fulfill romance or lust, and so on. Ultimately, the pattern of control is the ego's attempt to protect you from feeling alone or abandoned. It's a protection against the fear of losing its perceived control of reality.

Your ego likes to know what to anticipate so that you can more or less be prepared to deal with it. That provides feelings of comfort and supports the illusion that you are in charge. You can probably see that the ego patterns of comfort, security, and control are "kissing cousins."

## Resistance

If comfort, security, and control are "kissing cousins," a close relative to all of them is *resistance*. All three primary ego patterns often result in the experience of resistance. Resistance can be looked upon as a conditioned response of the ego designed to maintain the status quo, which is but another name for the comfort zone.

As we all know from experience, many of us resist exploring new territory. Sometimes resistance may masquerade as passivity through nonaction, thus undermining your stated purpose, intentions, and goals. Sometimes it's experienced as reluctance to expand or move forward beyond the perceived safety and security of your current habits, despite the fact that you are not achieving your expressed goals. Sometimes resistance is reflected in loss of focus through becoming distracted and consequently being thrown off purpose. And sometimes it manifests as reluctance to developing the levels of Loving Self-supportive discipline that would move you forward in fulfilling your goals, aspirations, and initiatives.

Usually, the underlying positive intention of the ego is that of protecting you from experiencing discomfort (such as you imagine will result from greater success, visibility, or responsibilities), some imagined catastrophe, perceived threats to survival, or fears of losing approval or love.

## Moving Forward

If there's one thing that will tend to propel you out of your comfort zone, it's daring to Awaken into Higher Consciousness, moving up on the Soul Line, and living within greater Awareness of the Spiritual Context. Such a journey takes you into uncharted territory—the frontiers of your own consciousness.

In our experience, fear of the unknown—be it expressed as comfort, security, control, or any other ego pattern—is the single dynamic that stops more people from moving ahead in their lives than any other factor. This is why it is so difficult for many people to break addictions and other habits that do not serve their aspirations. They are unwilling to be with their fear long enough to allow it to run its course. The familiarity of their habitual addictive behavior is stronger than their intention.

Now here's the good news. The secret of navigating the fear of the unknown is that you must be willing to run the experiment of venturing into the unknown, doing whatever it is that you are afraid of doing—all while being fully afraid of doing it. It is through this experiential process that you demonstrate to yourself that there really was nothing to be afraid of in the first place.

Probably my (Ron's) most vivid example of meeting my comfort zone goes back to my early thirties, when I had the desire to become a licensed pilot. After all, my best friend had achieved this goal, and if he could do it, surely I could too.

And so, one clear and sunny day, I drove to Ramapo Valley Airport in Westchester County just north of Manhattan, New York. I found myself climbing into a Cherokee 140 for my first lesson, which I shortly realized meant actually flying up into the air. I'm not sure just what exactly I thought we'd be doing, but somehow moving an aircraft from the ground to several thousands of feet in the air wasn't part of what I envisioned my first lesson to be!

As if I wasn't frightened enough, my instructor's first words to me, after we had climbed to altitude and were flying straight and level, were, "Okay, take over the controls."

"What?" I said. "I've never done this before. I don't know what to do."

"That's the point," he answered. "You don't have to do anything. Unlike driving a car, once you've set the plane up to fly straight and level, it will keep flying that way all by itself until you do something to change it. Pilot training is all about knowing what to do when you're ready to make a change."

What a concept. Of course, he was right. And at that point, I felt myself relax and begin to enjoy the experience. I literally experienced a shift in consciousness, and I began to diligently turn my attention to learning how the various control systems worked in conjunction with the gauges that told me some really important information, like what altitude I was flying. And, all the while, I was aware of the beauty that is ever present in a small plane flying at a relatively low altitude.

### *Venturing Higher*

By daring to consistently challenge your comfort zone, you'll discover that you're becoming a person whose fear has been gradually replaced by Courage, Trust, and a positive sense of awe and wonder. Once you realize that you simply do not know what the future holds—and you are at Peace with not knowing—you begin to experience a shift in Consciousness. It is at this point that you have transcended your ego's creation of a comfort zone and find yourself experiencing the Freedom of what we refer to as the Divine Unknowing.

Moving into this Awareness is a happy day, because the territory of the Divine Unknowing is the only place of Authentic Freedom any of us will ever find. It's a place of opportunity where we are free to live much more fulfilling lives. This is the motivation behind psychologist Piero Ferrucci's advice to "Eliminate something superfluous from your life. Break a habit. Do something that makes you feel insecure."

DIVINE UNKNOWING
*(freedom, creativity
inspiration)*

COMFORT ZONE
*(known and familiar
to the ego)*

The Authentic Self's Perspective

## Mary's Comfort Zone of Invisibility

Awakening provides a beautiful opportunity to come into cooperation with your humanness and your Divinity. I (Mary) would like to share here what for me was an enlightening experience of encountering my own resistance that surfaced when I unexpectedly ran into a deeply held comfort zone some years ago.

As a child I had polio and developed a muscle imbalance in my eyes that is known as strabismus (one eye was misaligned) as well as amblyopia (sometimes referred to as "lazy eye"). My parents, to whom I am eternally grateful, were proactive about my seeing an ophthalmologist regularly, who prescribed glasses and an occluder (black patch) to be worn over the eye with stronger vision. This practice was intended to get the so-called lazy eye to work, and it was going on during the time I was learning to read. Fortunately, it did not hamper me and I became an avid reader.

My mom would invite me to read out loud to her every morning before breakfast when she would style my hair for me—a process that easily could take a half hour or more. My mom and I read many wonderful books together. I'd read one page, and then she'd read one page as she arranged my hair. I so appreciate the inspired way she engaged me in reading wonderful stories that opened windows to worlds I did not yet consciously know, as she simultaneously nurtured me.

My parents were told that because of the nature of my particular condition, I did not have a good prognosis for the corrective eye surgery, so I lived with this condition well into my adulthood. I do remember another little girl in my first-grade class who had the surgery successfully, and I was quite saddened that I could not. (This was an opportunity for practicing Acceptance, although I did not know it at the time.)

After Ron and I moved to California to begin bringing forward our work offering programs in Spiritual Psychology, I found myself aware that my lazy eye was distracting to people, as they reported difficulty in telling where I was looking. I decided to explore the possibility of eye surgery and received a referral, scheduled an appointment, and met the surgeon. My suitability for the corrective surgery was favorably evaluated, and I was elated!

At the nurse's station, while scheduling a date for the surgery, I suddenly felt very faint. I leaned forward on the counter to keep myself from falling. The nurse took one look at me and said, "My dear, you better sit down." She came out from behind the counter, skillfully guiding me to a chair. I spent some period of time sipping water, holding a cold compress to my forehead, and breathing smelling salts. Ron and I left the office without scheduling the surgery.

As Ron drove me home, we both knew there was something deeper surfacing beyond simply scheduling a surgery. After all, fainting was not part of my standard behavioral repertoire when scheduling appointments! Suffice it to say, I had encountered my comfort zone, which resulted in a deep inner resistance to the surgery and whatever it represented. Given the depth of our psychological training and personal experiences of working our own inner process, Ron and I both recognized the possibility of a Spiritual opportunity. It was clear to us that further exploration was required before moving forward with eye surgery.

I decided it was wise to allow some time to pass and not push the river, so to speak, as the inner feedback/resistance had been very strong. After a couple of months, I did the deeper inquiry. It included an intensive inner process that began with me lovingly asking the part inside that had precipitated my almost fainting in the doctor's office what its purpose was. It replied, "Protection."

In exploring this further, my consciousness revealed that "not seeing" was protecting me from "being seen." Some part of me believed that if I couldn't see, I wouldn't be seen by others and that would keep me safe. At that point, I thanked the part inside for its intention to keep me safe and asked if together we could explore other possible forms of protection. Receiving an affirmative response, we continued.

Three possible forms of protection were suggested. The first was gaining weight. I let the inner part know that this was not an option I would like to utilize and asked for other possibilities. The second option was shown to me as an image of myself being completely surrounded, enfolded, and protected by an angel's wings radiating a beautiful white Light. I liked this option very much. The third option was similar: being embraced by the Unconditional Loving of the Madonna, Mother Mary.

During this process, many tears were shed, and I engaged in deep Compassionate Self-Forgiveness for buying into the deep-seated misunderstanding that if I couldn't see, I also could not be seen. I experienced myself being flooded with Loving as I let go of this old story that had been unconscious to me for so many years.

When I completed this inner process (which went on for some time), I experienced deep Peace and relaxation. In my Heart, I knew I was now ready for the eye surgery. However, I allowed some months to pass as I intuitively felt it would be wise to allow my consciousness time to recalibrate at the new level. I also intended to select a different surgeon so there was no associational linkage to the earlier experience.

Some time later, Spirit brought Ron a client who was a well-known ophthalmologist. One day after a session, Ron told him about my condition and asked if he could suggest a referral. He certainly could and did—providing a personal referral to the world's preeminent surgeon for the required procedure.

I'll simply say that when I visited the surgeon in San Francisco and went through a thorough examination of my eyes, I found myself in a state of Joy. I saw purple light everywhere. The inner alignment and cooperation present within my consciousness were palpable. Scheduling the surgery was a nonevent.

The surgical procedure itself took place under Grace with absolutely none of the possible side effects shared by the doctor's nurse during that office visit prior to the surgery. She had showed me pictures of bruised faces and bloodshot eyes, while also reporting that some patients experience double vision and a few become blind. I was crystal clear inside myself that these potential outcomes would not be my experience, and so I did not accept any of those negative implants.

When the doctor visited me before I checked out of the hospital, he told me I was his star patient. He didn't ask me what I had done, and I didn't volunteer anything other than my Gratitude.

More than 25 years later, my eyes remain in alignment and my vision has gradually improved with time.

This experience is an example of how a comfort zone gets established and is held in place by limiting beliefs stored in the ego. It also serves as a reference point for me of addressing my resistance to the surgery by coming into cooperation within myself. I was willing to do the inner work necessary to heal the limiting beliefs that were the self-imposed prison bars of my uncomfortable comfort zone of invisibility.

Moving ahead with the surgery required moving out of my comfort zone and surrendering into the Divine Unknowing. It was a courageous leap of faith. It was a process of entrusting myself to Spirit—holding an intention for the best possible outcome while also trusting that the results of the surgery would be for my Highest Good, knowing that I had done the inner work to prepare myself to receive Healing Grace.

I truly experienced the moment heralded by these words attributed to Anaïs Nin: "And the day came when the risk to remain tight in a bud was more painful than the risk it took to blossom."

## THIS CHAPTER'S PRACTICE

### *Stepping Free of Your Comfort Zone*

Reflect on a typical day in your life and notice the habitual ways you have of doing things. Consider changing some things: take a different route to work, eat different foods, exercise in a new way, or learn something new. We encourage you in choosing to consciously shift one or more behavior patterns.

If you're feeling adventurous, choose to do a minimum of one new practice that you perceive is outside your current comfort zone. For example, we know several people who, when challenged in this way, went skydiving. Almost anything that is outside of what you are comfortable doing will suffice—keeping in mind, of course, the importance of taking care of yourself. And then, of course, do it!

Write about your experiences in your journal—especially those experiences where you felt afraid and how you felt after doing the thing you were afraid of doing.

## INTENTION

I am bringing forward the strength of my Heart, daring to take specific steps designed to assist me in transcending the familiarity of my comfort zone and moving into the Freedom of the Divine Unknowing.

CHAPTER 13

# THE MOTHER OF
# ALL CHOICES

*"Man must cease attributing his problems to his environment
and learn again to exercise . . . personal responsibility."*

— ALBERT SCHWEITZER

In the previous chapter, we discussed the challenges inherent in moving from your comfort zone into the Divine Unknowing, the most powerful of these being the fear that emerges when you dare attempt the transition. And nowhere is this challenge more prevalent than in Choosing to accept personal responsibility for your internal process, independent of outer situations and circumstances. We call this the Mother of All Choices.

On the positive side, it is by so choosing that you are empowering yourself with a personal "get out of jail free" card that opens the door through which you have an opportunity to liberate yourself from the pain of emotional suffering, including blame, shame, judgment, guilt, and hurt feelings.

Choosing to take personal responsibility for what's going on inside of you is like your own Day of Deliverance—it's the day your Authentic Empowerment begins. Each time you bring forward the Strength of your Heart and choose to take dominion within your own consciousness, you've achieved a personal victory. You become a Spiritual Warrior; you recognize that emotional reactivity and judgment are nothing more than feedback mechanisms that let you know there's an opportunity available for Healing, personal liberation, and Awakening.

As you strengthen your "taking dominion" muscles, you'll begin to realize that all the events of your life are neutral. We certainly understand that some of them are more challenging than others. What's essential to know is that the thoughts you project, and the story that you've created about yourself, become a powerful attractor field that draws to you experiences that validate and thus reinforce your beliefs and your resulting story.

Now here's the thing! You, and only you, have the inner authority to change your story. This fact becomes eminently clear as you recognize that YOU, and YOU ALONE, are the author! As you change your story by taking responsibility for your inner environment and applying Loving to the places inside where there is hurt or disturbance of any kind, you Awaken more fully into your Essential Loving Nature. In so doing, you transform your inner environment—and, lo and behold, your outer experiences follow suit.

### The Challenge of "UnPeace" While Traveling as an Ambassador of Peace

One of my biggest opportunities for exercising my (Mary's) "taking dominion" muscles came many years ago when Ron and I traveled to Israel and Egypt with our Spiritual Teacher and 200 others as ambassadors of Peace. I had prepared diligently for the trip, getting all the recommended prescriptions and shopping for pretty little outfits such as a wide-brimmed sun hat to help me avoid bad hair days, a lovely feminine parasol to protect my head and face from the sun, sturdy walking shoes to wear by day, and sexy sandals to wear by night. I even purchased little white gauze gloves at the behest of my inner guidance while having no idea of their purpose or why I might need them—and, believe it or not, I was sooooo grateful to have them as I walked through Hezekiah's Tunnel in Jerusalem in hip-high water and navigated the low, narrow passages to and from what is aptly named "the Pit" inside the Great Pyramid at Giza.

Finally, the appointed day arrived. We flew to Amsterdam, where we spent the night for my birthday, and the next day flew to Tel Aviv. Upon arrival we made our way laboriously through customs and then, late that night, traveled by bus to a kibbutz on the Sea of Galilee. It was late when we arrived, and so it was quickly to bed.

To my surprise, I awoke the next morning cloaked in basic black dread, wanting in the worst way to go home. I quickly realized that I had best tell Ron, as he would no doubt pick up on my energy and wonder what on earth was going on with me.

Summoning my honesty, I reluctantly shared, "I'm feeling basically dreadful . . . And I'm also feeling like I'd like to go immediately to the nearest airport and go home." I paused, then followed with, "I'm only going to talk about this once (now), as I don't think it's going to be helpful for me to be whining and complaining about this throughout the trip."

Ron gave me a hug and words of encouragement. I suggested that he go ahead to breakfast, and I would come along as soon as I could prepare myself to muster smiles and small talk. I was still contemplating the pros and cons of staying versus beating a hasty retreat to the airport.

I decided to walk toward the dining room in a nearby building. Then, in the lobby, I sat down to further consider my options. I realized I *could* choose to sink deeper into the unexplained fear and foreboding and suffer the self-victimization of "I'm upset because . . ." for the rest of the trip—a very unpleasant prospect, particularly because our trip was to be 30 days long. I knew that would mean looking out through judgmental eyes and finding something to blame for my feelings. This was a recipe for a miserable time for myself, and very likely for those around me. I swallowed hard and my eyes moistened with tears as I considered my plight. I was 10,000 miles from home on a trip I'd been preparing to take for more than a year.

On the other hand, I could summon the courage to make the Mother of All Choices by taking responsibility for what was going on inside of me. After all, nothing catastrophic had happened. I realized I didn't even have a justifiable excuse—a good "because" for the way I was feeling! I decided that this latter choice would definitely be the High Ground.

I began flooding the place inside that was feeling doomed and down with Loving, remembering the Spiritual Psychology Principle, "How you relate to the issue is the issue," and more specifically, "How you relate to yourself while you go through the issue is the issue." After a few minutes of breathing Loving into the place in my solar plexus that was feeling foreboding, and talking with myself in a sweet and encouraging way, I began to feel a bit better. I knew I'd need to do a lot more of this by way of bringing Acceptance and Peace to the place inside that was experiencing "endarkenment." Making this Self-Honoring Choice was a beginning.

At that moment, I heard, "How are you, Mary?" Recognizing my Teacher's voice, I turned to greet him, flashed him a tenuous smile, and told him I was all right. I quickly got up and gave him a hug. He put his arm around me, and together we walked into the dining room. To me, this encounter with him was very affirming and helped me hang in there during what was to turn out to be a rather daunting, yet profoundly transformational journey. Believe me, the opportunities for taking dominion in my own consciousness took place on a daily basis throughout the trip.

## Trading Justification for Empowerment

What we find extremely interesting is the variety of situations and circumstances that people share in which they experience emotional disturbance. And even more amazing is how their disturbance is almost always "justified"—there's always some "because." The author Werner Erhard was fond of pointing out this phenomenon when he remarked that, "I never met a man who was just late." Had he been in the context of Spiritual Psychology, he might have said, "I never met a man who was just upset."

As we move into the next few chapters, we'll encourage you in enhancing your willingness to take 100 percent responsibility for what's going on within your own consciousness. This one step will open you to a whole new world of choices that we'll be sharing with you as we move forward together.

### *Freedom through Accepting Personal Responsibility*

You can use these empowering steps to support yourself in making the Mother of All Choices. You're no doubt well aware that life tends to bring you situations and circumstances that trigger reactivity. So we suggest you choose a period of time (two weeks works nicely) to *neutrally observe* instances when you experience any emotional disturbance. As one occurs, note the situation, what happened, and your disturbance. When you have sufficient time, write your responses to each of the following steps in your journal. (Many people do this in the evening.)

It's not necessary to experience a big upset in order to find value in this process. Often seemingly subtle disturbances provide rich opportunities for Healing and letting go. And here's some good news. The more you work with this process, the easier it gets and the more facile you become at the process of taking dominion within your own consciousness.

Step 1: Identify a situation where you found yourself experiencing emotional upset and blaming someone else for what happened and your reaction. What happened? How did you react?

Step 2: Provide a safe and sacred space in which you give yourself permission to honestly share your experience and feelings using "I'm upset because . . ." statements. Give your feelings a voice and write out what they have to say.

Step 3: Move into Compassion for yourself and your feelings. In being with yourself, use Soul-Centered skills such as

Seeing the Loving Essence, Heart-Centered Listening, and Perception Checking.

For example, you might write something like, *"I hear you, and I hear how challenging this experience is or was for you."*

Step 4: Encourage yourself in accepting responsibility for what's happening inside of you by separating the triggering situation (the outer event) from your feelings/upset (the inner experience).

For example, you might write something like, *"Considering the possibility that my emotional reactions—my feelings—were not caused by what happened, is there another way I might look at this experience and my feelings about it?"*

Step 5: Gently work with coming into Acceptance: Acceptance of what is (what happened), Acceptance of your feelings, and Acceptance of the others involved.

For example, you might write something like, *"What happened really triggered me, and I'm still upset about it. And I can accept that I'm upset and that I experienced judgment of myself, what happened, the other person(s) involved, and the situation itself. And I'm choosing to move into Acceptance of myself and my feelings and the experience I had. I know that I'm a caring human being who is learning how to take responsibility for my emotional upset regardless of what happened."*

Step 6: Gently remind yourself that the part inside that feels angry or hurt is not all of who you are, and that by applying your own Loving to the place inside that hurts, you can facilitate emotional Healing. Remember, how you relate to yourself while you go through the issue is the issue!

For example, you might write something like, *"I'm consciously choosing to move into my Heart, getting in touch with the Loving that resides there, and gently breathing that Loving into the place inside my body where I experience judgment and upset. I'm allowing myself to experience Compassion for that part of me that feels hurt and upset about what happened."*

Step 7: Support yourself in recognizing that by Accepting Responsibility for your inner experience, which is an act of empowerment, you are embracing a foundational building block essential for issue resolution and Healing—and in service to your Awakening.

For example, you might write something like, *"I recognize that by Accepting that my feelings are within my domain and are not caused by others, I am choosing to shift from the victim consciousness of blaming others to a consciousness of empowerment. In fact, I see it as an act of Loving empowerment for myself when I acknowledge that someone else did not cause my feelings of hurt and rejection, and that this upset is an opportunity for my own Healing."*

Step 8: Acknowledge yourself for your courage and willingness to experiment with taking responsibility for your own emotional reactions, and to apply Loving to the place inside where there is hurt, emotional pain, and/or upset.

---

### INTENTION

I am bringing forward the Strength of my
Heart, Lovingly and Compassionately taking dominion within
my consciousness by making the Mother of All Choices—taking
responsibility for what's going on inside of me, especially when
I'm experiencing "I'm upset because . . ."

---

# CHAPTER 14

# FREEDOM THROUGH COMPASSIONATE SELF-FORGIVENESS

*"Forgiveness is the answer to the child's dream of a miracle by which what is broken is made whole again, what is soiled is again made clean."*

— DAG HAMMARSKJOLD

Now that you've had an opportunity to venture into the territory of the Divine Unknowing by exercising the Mother of All Choices and taking 100 percent responsibility for your internal experience independent of anything that's happening in your outer world, it's time to learn how to take the next, and perhaps most essential, step in your break for Freedom. And it has to do with *Forgiveness*.

## *The Importance of Forgiveness*

Ever wonder why Forgiveness is so important? In February 2014, we had the privilege of listening to Patrick Chamusso, who had been incarcerated with Nelson Mandela for the better part of 17 years at the Robben Island maximum-security prison in Cape

Town, South Africa. He was speaking to a group of students and alumni at a University of Santa Monica event.

Patrick talked about how Mandela stressed the importance of forgiveness. But it wasn't "forgiveness" as many of us understand that word—forgiveness for those who have done "bad" things to us. As Patrick so beautifully expressed it, along with an upward gesture of his hand from his heart, "You must take the pain out of your heart and let it go."

What does that really mean and how can we do that? Just what is the "pain" that we must release from our Heart, and how do we "let it go"?

We all resonated with the pain that Mandela was talking about as the suffering that automatically results within us whenever we engage in the process of judgment—which is blaming, making wrong, condemning, vilifying, and so on. Think of it this way. If you got a thorn in your hand from picking roses from a rose bush, would you be more concerned with blaming the rose bush or getting the thorn out of your hand?

Compassionate Self-Forgiveness is the process that releases the thorn from your hand. It dissolves judgments and brings a Healing balm of Loving to the places inside where emotional pain resides. Without this process, freedom from emotional suffering would be impossible. Once you uttered your first judgment, there would be no way to retract it. You'd exist eternally in a self-created hell where you'd erect buildings, rituals, and philosophies that all supported eradicating the dangers of rose bushes—none of which would do anything toward releasing the thorn. You'd be like the proverbial prodigal son, only you'd never find your way Home.

Compassionate Self-Forgiveness is your return ticket. It's the simplest and most effective way we know of returning Home—of being restored to your Heart and to the Awareness of the Loving that is your Essential Nature. This is so important that it's worth reviewing in a bit more detail.

### Why "Compassionate Self-Forgiveness"?

Complete Forgiveness means letting go of any and all judgments. By so doing, you literally move within your consciousness from the place of judging to the place of Loving through the Healing Power of Forgiving. You might think of it this way: *To travel from the land of judgment to the land of Loving, you ride on the train of Forgiveness.* In other words, it's a key for remembering who you truly are.

It's through the Healing action of Forgiving yourself for judging that you are liberated—not through the action of forgiving others for "causing" you pain. While forgiving someone else for doing something you perceive to be "bad" or "wrong" is surely a positive step in a healthy direction, can you see that inside yourself you are still holding a belief that what they did was "bad" or "wrong"? You are still engaged in the ego's way of thinking; when you so engage, you are simply entering into a more subtle level of judging.

And why *Compassionate* Self-Forgiveness? Because the word *Compassion* means to be with someone who is suffering—and to be *with* them in a Loving way. It is an action of the Heart. It is a way of Compassionately being *with* yourself when you are the one who is suffering. It's a good thing to keep in mind that you, just like everyone else, are really doing the best you know how to do given your Spiritual Curriculum. That realization immediately takes you to a place of Compassion, and Compassion makes the Forgiving process so much easier.

Remember, the emotional suffering you experience takes place in the ego-centered dimension operating in physical-world reality where you exist within the imprisoning duality of right and wrong as defined and perceived by you. In order to alleviate such suffering, consider how your current definitions and perceptions of reality —which lead to judgments of yourself and others—are at the root of your mental anguish and emotional suffering.

The good news is that you can experientially test this possibility and observe the results of your experiment. You can release the judgments, limiting beliefs, and misinterpretations of reality that you are holding; restore yourself to a place of Peace; and experience for yourself the degree to which your life changes—all through the method of Compassionate Self-Forgiveness.

## *The Process of Compassionate Self-Forgiveness*

Self-Forgiveness is a most powerful Healing process. It involves the inner action of moving into and experiencing Love and Compassion for yourself as well as for all Creation. It is the Cosmic Delete Button, an antidote to the pain and separation that result from passing judgment. More than words, Compassionate Self-Forgiveness is a process of releasing judgments that naturally results in the experience of Loving. It is a process in harmony with Awakening and recognizes that we are humans really doing the best we know how to do in any given moment, even though our performance sometimes falls short of our aspirations. Compassionate Self-Forgiveness provides a way of distinguishing, affirming, and experiencing the Loving Essence of who you are independent of your thoughts, feelings, and behavior.

One morning a few weeks ago, I (Mary) awakened with the awareness of a very old memory that had seeded many childhood terrors, including a fear of the dark. Throughout my childhood, when my mother and father would put me to bed, my last request to them each evening was, "Please leave the hall light on." My parents invariably granted my request, giving my small self (ego) a sense of safety, security, comfort, and control.

As the details of this memory surfaced, I realized how deeply fear had imprinted upon my consciousness and informed my life. I was experiencing a heaviness and waves of fog—not a good feeling. I began unraveling the memory and Forgiving myself for my judgments and misunderstandings such as, "I Forgive myself for judging myself as afraid of the unknown. I Forgive myself for judging myself as unsafe. I Forgive myself for judging myself as unprotected. I Forgive myself for forgetting that I am Divine."

The shift in my energy was instantaneous and profound. The heaviness and fog immediately lifted, revealing crystalline Clarity, a sense of Freedom, and deep Peace. I commented to Ron, "I feel sooooooo much better!" Though I have been practicing Compassionate Self-Forgiveness for many years, I became once again aware of its power and the powerful shifts in consciousness that flow from it. Another barrier that I had built against the Awareness of the Love that I Am was dissolved. I am forever grateful. I was reminded of this quote, attributed to Mark Twain, which is one of my favorites: "Forgiveness is the fragrance a violet sheds on the heel that has crushed it."

Ron and I have both been utilizing the Practice of Compassionate Self-Forgiveness for many years, and it has been life changing and consciousness altering. For me, it has been incredibly helpful when slogging through difficult times: visiting a historic Egyptian temple along the Nile and going into shock after passing through an ancient initiation site, exploring the inner and outer darkness of the Pit of the Great Pyramid at Giza, climbing down and back up a narrow and steep winding staircase inside the Physician's Tomb at Saqqara, facing a challenging illness, holding the Light for my Beloved Ron when he experienced open-heart surgery and extended recovery, the deaths of my beloved parents, and standing as a Spiritual Warrior during a two-year onslaught of negativity from an outside source. On and on it goes. I have truly learned experientially the Healing power of this Practice.

### Self-Compassion and Self-Acceptance through Compassionate Self-Forgiveness

In our work, we often experience many beautiful moments flowing from the Healing power of Compassionate Self-Forgiveness. Here's an example in which we had the privilege of witnessing of a lovely young woman moving from emotional upset and self-judgment to Self-Acceptance, Peace, and Joy.

This blessing took place as we were completing a culminating class weekend with second-year students who would soon be graduating from the University's Master's Program in Spiritual Psychology. The weekend was breathtaking in the Beauty and Fullness of

Spirit's Presence. The students' sharings were one exquisite High Note after another.

On Sunday morning, one student stood up in some upset about feedback she'd received from a few of her classmates about her class project, which was about feminine beauty and fashion. They'd expressed that they found her project to be superficial, materialistic, and not very spiritual. The experience triggered for her some deep material associated with what had been some of her deeply held "secret" judgments of herself and her stand for Beauty as less than spiritual. In that moment, however, the young woman began Compassionately Forgiving herself for judgments of herself as anything less than Beautiful just as she is—and then sat down.

Our head sound person—who's worked with us for years and is very "tuned in"—looked at Ron, who nodded back. Then, he immediately began playing a recording of Billy Joel singing "Just the Way You Are." Moments after the first chords were played, the entire class began singing along, gently swaying in their chairs, serenading not just the young woman who had shared but also themselves. We were all suddenly outside of time and space, experiencing the miraculous that occurs when Hearts open and the transcendent Power of Spirit pours in, bringing with it the experience of Oneness, Peace, Contentment, Acceptance, and Love.

We moved as a group into the Authentic Self level, where experiences of Love, Happiness, and Joy are all that is. The Radiant Beauty and absolute Peacefulness of their faces as they sang into the Great Silence are deeply etched in the memory of our Hearts. I (Mary) am forever grateful for this experience and doubt I will ever forget it.

## A Story of Radical Transformation through Compassionate Self-Forgiveness

Here's another beautiful example of a student's experience in daring to live into her Spiritual Curriculum. In one of the University's live classes, Ron shared: "One of the primary ways disturbance comes in is when you judge." One of the students truly heard this message with the ears of her Heart. She took Ron's words as her personal challenge to courageously move out of the experiences of the judgment-induced contraction and separation present within her consciousness. Ron's message had been reverberating within her for a month when she shared:

> *I have been in this process of Waking Up into the Awareness of how much darkness I've had in my life, my heart, and my body. I've really been struggling with feeling safe and free. What I've been noticing is that when I judge, it collapses my Universe. I get scared and start judging everything that's happening. As you can imagine, I shut down and my life shuts down. I'm unavailable to the Awareness of anything else.*
>
> *In response to Ron's statement, I made a decision that whenever I started to feel inner disturbance, I'd immediately take responsibility for that disturbance and begin engaging in Compassionate Self-Forgiveness. What I'm finding is that when I say "I Forgive," Oneness wraps around me and I experience Forgiving my judgments of myself, others, and the world; and Forgiving any misunderstandings for all time.*
>
> *My inner experience is that something inside of me keeps opening like a rose blossom, naturally revealing its full beauty. The Universal Love keeps growing and evolving inside me into the experience of Freedom, Peace, Acceptance, and Receiving. Whatever part of me thinks I'm not beautiful, whole, perfect, and meant to be right here, right now, I just let those judgments go. I forgive and I am restored to Peace, Acceptance, Self-Trust, and Awareness of the Love that I AM. Something changes within my body, within my consciousness; it's like I'm crossing a bridge.*

This woman's sharing demonstrates a high level of Ownership—of courageously choosing to take Responsibility for what was going on within her own consciousness—and she is experiencing the benefits of her choice. She's *experiencing* herself releasing the crystallized barriers that were the products of her judgments and misunderstandings. She's stopped trying to figure anything out and started allowing the energy to flow through by practicing Forgiveness . . . Acceptance . . . Compassion . . . Peace . . . Loving . . . And voilà—Freedom.

What's notable about this woman's beautiful experience is her Courageous Heart: Courageous in choosing to release her fears, Courageous in choosing to Compassionately Forgive herself for her judgments, and Courageous in choosing to expand into the Loving in the face of the ego's contraction.

It's been said that it takes great Courage to see the face of God. We have found this to be true, for no matter how many books you have read, seminars you've attended, and ideas you've contemplated, Awakening occurs when you muster the Strength of Heart to begin implementing what you are learning. When you dare to open your mind and Heart to new ways of Seeing and Being, and experience the results for yourself, then you will experience Awakening.

The transformation and liberation this student experienced, are here for you, too—simply waiting for you to courageously answer the Call to Love.

When all is said and done, do you know what we experience as the greatest Blessing? The Awareness that inside the Lighthouse of each of our Hearts, the Light is always on, welcoming us Home— and it always has been on.

That's what Awakening means: becoming aware of that Inherent Inner Light that is always on!

## THIS CHAPTER'S PRACTICES

This chapter contains two Practices. The three keys will help you move into the quality of Compassion inside yourself. Practicing any or all of them prior to doing Compassionate Self-Forgiveness will assist you in deepening the process and enhancing your experience.

We encourage you to practice the Seven Steps for Experiencing Compassionate Self-Forgiveness at least once a day for the next few weeks. Quite honestly, we recommend that you practice them for the rest of your life!

## Three Keys for Moving into Compassion

You can choose to do one or all of these tools at any time. Over the years, we have found them to work very well for moving into Compassion, as they tend to evoke experiences that are Heart opening. They are ways of moving into your Heart and connecting with your Loving; it's easy to do once you get the hang of it.

Key 1: Think of a child or anyone else you Love. (Pets count!)

Key 2: Close your eyelids and slowly take in a nice deep breath . . . and then slowly let it out. Repeat this rhythm, and on the in-breath think *Peace* . . . And on the out-breath think *Love* . . . Continue this Practice for a few minutes.

Key 3: Think of your favorite place in nature in which you experience timelessness and a deep sense of Peace and well-being.

## Seven Steps for Experiencing Compassionate Self-Forgiveness

You can use these Seven Steps for Experiencing Compassionate Self-Forgiveness to assist yourself in dissolving inner disturbance through releasing ego-based judgment and emotional upsets, thereby restoring yourself to your Essential Nature of Loving.

We encourage you to write the questions and your responses to each question in your journal. Write the experiences that triggered judgments, your Compassionate Self-Forgiveness statements, and your experience doing the process. Some people like to do this process in the evening before they go to bed. It becomes a kind of evening review and a process of letting go. You may just find that you also sleep better!

Step 1: Choose a situation that has triggered emotional upset within you, whether currently or at an earlier time.

Step 2: Allow yourself to experience and express your feelings. (If you are someone who is challenged in this area, you may find it helpful to skip ahead and read Chapter 16, particularly the section on Writing and Burning.)

Step 3: Realizing that beneath all emotional upset are judgments seeking resolution, allow yourself to identify and explore any judgments you may have placed against yourself or others regarding this situation. (Clue: What did you find "wrong" in the situation or in what someone else said or did?)

Step 4: From a Compassionate place within, gently move into Compassionate Self-Forgiveness. Here is some coaching regarding effective language for doing this process:

- You can do Compassionate Self-Forgiveness of judgments for behaviors actually done, which you are working to bring to peaceful resolution and Acceptance. For example, "I forgive myself for judging myself for all the times I engaged in lying and deception."

- You can do Compassionate Self-Forgiveness for your limiting beliefs or misinterpretations of reality. For example, "I forgive myself for buying into the belief that it's selfish to ask for what I want," or "I forgive myself for buying into the belief that because my father left me when I was a child, that means I am unlovable."

- You can do Compassionate Self-Forgiveness for the negative attributions you've placed against yourself. For example, "I forgive myself for judging myself as wrong, unkind, unloving, insensitive, controlling, etc."

**Note:** The same applies to judgments you've placed against others. For example, "I Forgive myself for judging [*name*] as wrong, bad, selfish, inconsiderate, unkind, unloving, controlling, etc." Notice that you are Forgiving yourself for judging yourself *as*, and not for *being*. If you say, for instance, *"being* wrong," you are actually reinforcing the notion that you *are* wrong.

Step 5: Focusing your Awareness in your Heart, write or say out loud your Compassionate Self-Forgiveness statements so that all levels of your consciousness hear them. Express them from your Heart.

Step 6: Support yourself in being thorough by working with Compassionate Self-Forgiveness for each of the judgments or misinterpretations of reality previously identified. An upward shift in your energy is an indicator that your Self-Forgiveness is complete.

Step 7: When complete, acknowledge and appreciate yourself for your commitment to your Awakening and your courage and willingness to engage in the process of Compassionate Self-Forgiveness.

## INTENTION

I am accelerating my Awakening through cultivating the Practice of Compassionate Self-Forgiveness whenever I am aware of judgments and their accompanying emotional charge. I am in service to restoring myself to my Loving—releasing the barriers that block me from the Awareness of the Loving that I am. And by so doing, I am remembering Who I Am.

# CHAPTER 15

# UNRESOLVED ISSUES AREN'T IN THE WAY— THEY ARE THE WAY!

*"You were born with wings. Why prefer to crawl through life?"*

— Attributed to Rumi

To the quote that starts this chapter, we would add, "Awakening will set you free. Prepare to soar on the Wings of Love."

At this point, you may be feeling annoyed, irritated, or downright outraged. "What do you mean, unresolved issues aren't *in* the way, they *are* the way? What kind of outrageous nonsense is that? My issues, to say nothing of the issues of people I know, rear their ugly heads periodically. This causes me stress and distress and basically mucks up my life. I'm so tired of them. How can my anger, disappointment, frustration, fear, sadness, grief, hurt feelings, and judgments of myself, others, or this crazy world possibly be of any value? All they do for me is cause me suffering. How can they possibly be *the way*? The way to what?"

We hear you! I (Mary) remember reading Plato's famous "Allegory of the Cave" in *The Republic* as an 18-year-old. In the allegory, Plato describes a group of prisoners who are chained in such a way that they are facing a wall of a cave. They cannot move their heads, so all they see are shadows of things passing in front of a fire burning behind them. The shadows are as close as the prisoners come to experiencing reality, and they believe that what they are seeing is real.

In the class discussion regarding the allegory, the point was made that we are all like the prisoners, not seeing reality and making up in our minds what's real based on shadows. I recall feeling quite annoyed with the ideas that I was creating my reality and responsible for my life. In my annoyance, I vehemently thought to myself: *If I'm creating my reality, I'd sure do a lot better job than this!* My annoyance in combination with that emphatic declaration actually motivated me to learn more.

Now, many years later, I'm so grateful for the seeds that were planted by Plato. My subsequent experiences presented me with spiritual convergences—opportunities that turned me around, freeing me from a shadow existence as a prisoner in a dimly lit cave of my own creation. Eventually, I gratefully Awakened from my sleepwalking existence in which I was dreamily fighting shadowy windmills, those illusions created by the projections of my mind and emotions, misunderstanding all I saw.

Fortunately Spirit had other plans for me, and I began Awakening into the Light of the Spiritual Context. I've never forgotten the painful emotions associated with the deep sense of separation I experienced. Those trials evoked deep Compassion and a Calling within my Heart to assist others in freeing themselves from the shackles that restrict and limit Awareness of Spiritual Reality.

### *Further Principles of Spiritual Psychology*

You've probably noticed that even considering the idea of the Spiritual Context introduced in Chapter 1 invites a radical change in perception about who you are and what you're doing here on the planet. Reviewing the following 11 Principles of Spiritual Psychology invites you more deeply into that Context—opening a doorway to liberation. Read through them slowly; perhaps even read them out loud.

- The nature of God is Love.

- We are not human beings with Souls; we are Souls *using* a human experience for the purpose of Awakening.

- Since we are all a part of God, our Essential Nature also is Love—and we have the opportunity of *knowing* our Loving nature experientially, Here and Now.

- Earth functions as a school for Spiritual Awakening, meaning Conscious Awareness of the first three Principles above. Everyone registers for their specific Curriculum.

- Your Earth School or Spiritual Curriculum consists largely of Healing unresolved issues residing in your consciousness. It also includes opportunities for service, sharing your gifts, and living into your Heartfelt dreams.

- Unresolved issues are anything that disturbs your Peace.

- Unresolved issues are not bad; they're simply part of your Spiritual Curriculum.

- Unresolved issues are blessings, as they are opportunities for Healing and Awakening.

- The work of Healing, or resolving unresolved issues, is spiritual work and is a major aspect of what Spiritual Awakening is all about.

- One of your greatest opportunities for Awakening occurs when your school is in session—i.e., when your unresolved issues (upsets) surface.

- Healing is the application of Loving to the places inside that hurt or suffer; or Healing is the "flooding with Loving" of all the places inside that hurt or suffer, thereby dissolving them.

"Holy wow!" you might be saying to yourself. "I get it! Do you really mean that I can learn to use my upsets and unresolved issues as stepping stones—as rungs on the ladder of my Spiritual Awakening?"

*"Yes,"* we agree, *"that's exactly what we mean!"*

"Thank God! I knew there had to be a pony in here somewhere. Do you actually mean it? Can you give me an example of how someone really used an unresolved issue in service to their Healing and Awakening?"

*"Indeed we can."*

## A Courageous Woman's Story of Liberation: Vertigo—the Tip of the Iceberg

Here are the highlights of a sharing we had with a courageous 37-year-old woman who, for many years, had been experiencing what she described as "stuckness" in moving forward professionally. She shared that she had spent years moving from one career path to another—each time experiencing disappointment when she found her choice wasn't really in alignment with the Calling of her Heart. Simultaneously she was baffled and frustrated by the spinning sensations of vertigo that reoccurred each time she attempted to address her career goals and dreams. Whenever she started creating a Living Vision for her career (a tool we use in our live classes) she would experience extreme vertigo, which in turn triggered terror of losing control.

*Susan:* "My name is Susan and I've been struggling a lot with the Ideal Scenes and the Living Vision [processes for Co-Creating the future]. I think the struggle with it is that I've come to a place of not being really sure of who I am and who I thought I knew myself to be. This is not who I'm finding that I am now. So every time I start to do a Living Vision, I'm getting extreme vertigo. It's difficult to continue to work my process when that vertigo is so scary."

Susan wanted to become a professional life coach, and the vertigo was the worst when she attempted to move in that direction. She felt very stuck.

*Susan:* "Until recently I thought of myself as having it all figured out. Like, I had a plan and I had a career. I did all the steps—all the right things. I think that I want to be everything for everybody or have life all figured out. I want to have the career figured out, and have the right money in the savings account, and have the right Roth—and all these things.

"And what I'm finding is, as I've leaned into that, I just feel almost like I'm dying a little bit. I've struggled with suicidal thoughts. I'm doing all these things, but the more that I do, the less alive I feel. So I'm feeling now that this 'me' isn't real. I feel more alive when it's a little messier, and I don't have it all figured out. I'm thinking of taking a year off and spending the money that I've saved. That's what I feel like I really want to do. It makes me feel alive, but that's not at all what I thought my path was. I feel like I've been doing different versions of that same plan."

At this point we reflected to her that it seemed to us that she was being presented with a beautiful opportunity to really listen to the Calling of her Heart; to truly hear and honor that deeper place inside that was yearning for something more: more in the dimension of Meaning, Purpose, and Fulfillment—living into greater Freedom and Authenticity, trusting the Wisdom of her own Heart.

As we explored her yearning for Freedom and Inner Peace, Susan began to cry, overwhelmed by the feelings of fear and the physical disorientation of the vertigo.

*Susan:* "I just feel tired from the struggle of it and trying to figure it out. I do feel that sense of terror. And I think that's kind of the dichotomy inside: there is a real desire for the Freedom and real yearning to honor the Calling of my Heart. But also a real terror, and I'm scared to let go into unknowing."

### Susan's Self-Created Prison of Guilt, Unworthiness, and Self-Punishment

At this point, we asked Susan a key question: "Are there any things that have gone on in your life where you have felt either held hostage or imprisoned?"

*Susan:* "Yeah, for a long time. When I was in high school, my brother was killed in a car accident. I thought that it was my fault, and so I just took that to mean that I had kind of failed as a human being. I wasn't worth anything, and I just felt like that idea of myself has really kept me stuck."

We invited Susan to share more: "What happened? How did this happen? How did you get the idea that somehow it was your fault?"

*Susan:* "Growing up I was very shy and I just wanted to please everybody. I wanted everything to be really smooth. My older brother needed a lot of my parents' attention. He was diabetic, and he experimented with drugs and alcohol, and so I thought, *I can be helpful if I'm just not any trouble. I will get good grades and I'll do all the right things so my parents won't need to worry about me.* I felt like they had their hands full with him, so I always went along and just said, 'Yes. I will do this.' I made my own lunches—anything to make it easier.

"My brother was struggling with his blood sugar, and he got in a car accident. He came home and said to me, 'I need you to take me to get my car fixed.' And for the first time I said no, and I just unleashed this lifetime of frustration, of feeling ignored by my parents, and I told him how selfish he was. I was so mad that I did not even let him talk. I just spewed out all these things. And then I slammed my door, and the next day I got up early, and I went and took the bus to go to high school rather than ride with him. I was still really mad, you know, so upset with all the feelings that were coming up.

"So that day at lunch, I saw him in the hall and I was standing at my locker and he was coming over to me, like he wanted to say something, but I was still mad. He could see my message was, 'Not yet.' As he was coming toward me, I turned my back, and that was the last I ever saw him. He was killed on his way home.

"I thought, *If I had just said yes to take him to get his truck fixed, he wouldn't have been in the car that day,* and *Who was I to leave him with all that?* I really felt that I'd hurt his Soul . . . that he had passed on, and in doing so he was left with a lot of my anger. I just felt like I couldn't undo that. That's what made me begin to ask the question, 'Who am I? Who am I? Who am I?' I'd watched movies about inmates that are on death row, and they had gotten a better last day than I had given my brother."

At this point in our conversation, we reflected to Susan: "We hear that you've really been carrying this guilt, and that part of the pattern is that you became very reliant, self-sufficient, self-contained, and very concerned with doing the correct thing or the right thing."

Susan, who was standing, expressed that the vertigo was intensifying and said, "I just need to hang onto the chair."

We coached Susan: "There's a tremendous opportunity for letting go of the judgments and misinterpretations, the guilt and self-punishment—for letting go of the scripted life that you have led in order to not be a burden, to not make any waves, to not have any needs, to really just be self-reliant and take care of everything yourself. And to let go of the judgments that it was your fault and that you needed to suffer or pay in some way for what happened between you and your brother."

Susan responded: "That resonates, 'scripted life.' I feel like that."

We continued coaching Susan: "You know, I can appreciate the challenge inside of you, because when you came to a place where you'd had enough, and you spoke up, the way things flowed led you to conclude that somehow his death was your fault. That conclusion put you into a restrictive scripted life. And yet your attempting to live that scripted life has been an experience of such misery and confinement, a kind of imprisonment with no Joy, with no sense of fulfillment or meaning, or purpose, or fun."

## Susan Speaks with Her Brother's Soul

Below is the dialogue we shared with Susan where she connected with her brother's Soul and began to heal old wounds.

*Susan:* "I'm really getting that. It hasn't been fun, and there's been no Joy. I think that is the terror that if I free myself, or express myself really authentically, something really bad is going to happen again."

*Mary:* "I really hear you. And so that was the conclusion that you drew at that time. I can really understand that conclusion—as a young girl in high school having her brother pass suddenly, tragically, and with things unresolved between the two of you. Would you be open to speaking with your brother's Soul?"

*Ron:* "So if you were speaking with him, what would you want to ask him?"

*Susan:* "I would want to ask if I hurt him."

*Mary:* "And you can ask him. Let's inwardly ask that his Soul Essence be present with you here and now in service to your Healing, in service to your liberation, in service to clarifying this, for the Highest Good. So I encourage you to ask him, 'Did I hurt you?'"

*Ron:* "You don't have to ask it out loud; you can do it inwardly if you want, if that will be easier for you."

*Susan:* "So I am asking for my brother's Soul to come forward to speak to me, and what I would want to know is: Did I hurt you? And has your Soul been in pain because of how I left you?"

*Ron:* "And what does he answer?"

*Susan:* "I feel it more than I hear it. The feeling is more of a Loving embrace; he's really holding me. I just feel like I've been wanting that—that hug from my brother, for so long, and seeking it in many different ways. This is the first time I really felt it."

*Mary:* "I so encourage you in receiving it."

*Susan:* I'm just getting that there is no hurt and there is no pain. There's only Loving."

*Mary:* "Yes. I encourage you to take that in fully—into all levels of your consciousness, into every cell in your body. Is there anything else that you would like to say to him?"

*Susan:* "I think I had thought that I would want to say that I am sorry, but now, in that space, it just doesn't make sense to say that. It's just 'I love you.' And while I feel his Presence, I miss him."

### Susan's Compassionate Self-Forgiveness: Dissolving Guilt, Grief, and "Stuckness"

*Mary:* "This experience—what a Blessing—what a gift. You can call your brother's Soul forward at any time. You can call his Soul present. And I encourage you in this beautiful opportunity, in the Presence of the Power of the Love, to let go of the judgments. 'I forgive myself for buying into the misunderstanding that I was responsible for my brother's death, and the misunderstanding that I caused his Soul pain and suffering.'"

*Susan:* "I forgive myself for buying into the misunderstanding that I had caused my brother's Soul pain. And I forgive myself for buying in to the belief that I had failed at being human—that I had failed in my life. I forgive myself for judging myself as having failed, and as a failure. I forgive myself for judging myself as responsible for my brother's death."

*Mary:* "What are you experiencing inside yourself, Susan?"

*Susan:* "I feel like a weight has lifted. I feel so much lighter."

*Ron:* "And while you are at it, is there any message your brother has for you?"

*Susan:* "He just said, 'Be free. Go. Go fly. It's okay.' The quality that I picked from day one of this class, that was just there inside of me, was Lighthearted. And I just feel like I have not been Light-Hearted. I get that now: I just have a really Light Heart.

"I forgive myself for assigning myself a rigidly scripted life because I thought that that was the way. I forgive myself for assigning myself the penance of a heavy Heart."

*Mary:* "And what's the truth?"

*Susan:* "And the truth is that the only way to be is to be me. And the truth is I didn't hurt anybody."

*Mary:* "No."

*Susan:* "I am simply Loving."

*Ron:* "You were doing your best at the time, given your conditioning, experience, and Spiritual Curriculum."

*Susan:* "I was doing my best."

*Mary:* "And you are doing your best."

*Susan:* "And I am doing my best."

*Mary:* "Yes. So is there any other Forgiveness—anything else that you would like to let go of?"

*Susan:* "I forgive myself for judging myself as not enough. I forgive myself for judging myself as unworthy. I forgive myself for judging myself as really bad, and I forgive myself for judging myself as being behind. I forgive myself for judging myself as less than who I am. I forgive myself for judging myself as me."

*Mary:* "And what does that last statement mean?"

*Susan:* "It means that as I was going into my Authentic Self over these last three or four months, I was judging myself for doing that, because I thought, *You are going to do it again: you are going to really hurt somebody.*"

*Mary:* "And so, 'I also forgive myself for buying into the misunderstanding that if I live free, if I express the Authenticity of who I am, that some catastrophe will happen and others will be hurt.'"

*Susan:* "Yeah. I forgive myself for buying into the belief that if I live free, others will be hurt."

*Mary:* "Do you want to say that one again?"

*Susan:* "I forgive myself for buying into the belief that if I live free, others will be hurt. And the truth is, in being me and in being free, there is just Love."

*Mary:* "That is the truth. So one of the things you said earlier is that you wanted permission. So inside yourself, have you received permission?"

*Susan:* "Yes. I feel like I don't need to ask now."

*Mary:* "No, you have received it."

*Susan:* "Yeah."

*Mary:* "It's given."

*Susan:* "Yeah. Thank you."

Susan subsequently successfully completed the two-year Master's Degree Program in Spiritual Psychology and a seven-month Advanced Program in Soul-Centered Professional Coaching. We spoke with her recently, and she shared that she has gone on to do groundbreaking work in her state in the area of consulting and coaching focused on suicide prevention with teens and young people, and she is Director of the Suicide Prevention Coalition for her county. She has spoken to many clubs, businesses, organizations, colleges, and universities sharing her own story of Healing from suicidal thoughts and ideations; she has also been a panelist, keynote speaker, and guest lecturer. She is clear that making a difference for teens and college students is the heart of her work. Susan is now living the professional life that, at the time of this courageous Healing work, was only a dim dream held in the deep recess of her Heart.

Inspirational? Yes! Transformational? Another resounding yes! Available to you? Yes!

We began this chapter with Plato's "Allegory of the Cave," and we'd like to complete it with this evocative anonymous quote that seems so fitting: "We can easily forgive a child who is afraid of the dark; the real tragedy of life is when men are afraid of the Light."

## THIS CHAPTER'S PRACTICE

We hope that Susan's courageous work has inspired you and that you're ready to roll up your sleeves in bringing forward the Strength of Your Heart and Self-Compassion, and letting go of judgments, misunderstandings, and painful emotions that have held you in the crystallization, limitation, and suffering of your unresolved issue.

### Healing an Unresolved Issue

Your unresolved issues truly are vehicles you can use for your Awakening. It is a game changer to give voice to those experiences that you have not yet brought to a place of Peace and resolution inside yourself, and engage in Compassionate Self-Forgiveness.

We encourage you to write about an experience that you recognize as unresolved inside of you. Write from a place of self-honesty and vulnerability. Allow adequate time and a space that provides privacy. When you're ready, identify your judgments and limiting beliefs. Then move into Compassionate Self-Forgiveness, letting them go into the Light.

You, too, can experience greater Freedom as you choose to let go of painful memories and judgments, moving you into the Awareness of your already Loving Heart and freeing you to move forward in your life.

## INTENTION

I am bringing forward the Strength of my Heart,
courageously conducting and experiencing my life as
a magical opportunity for restoring myself to the
Awareness of my True Nature—the Presence of Love.
I am using my unresolved issues as stepping-stones—
rungs on the ladder of my Spiritual Awakening.
I am Forgiving myself, as I am remembering Who I Am—
a Divine Being using my human experience
in service to my Awakening.

# CHAPTER 16

# TIME-OUT FOR ADULTS

*"Holding on to anger is like grasping a hot coal with the intent of throwing it at someone else. You are the one who gets burned."*

— ATTRIBUTED TO BUDDHA

When involved in the process of Awakening, as you're likely well aware of by now, it's a good idea to have a variety of tools in your toolbox so that you are as prepared as possible for whatever may be needed. After all, if there's one thing you can count on, it's that your ego will use just about any excuse to avoid the process and thus maintain the status quo. One of its favorite ploys is feeding you the message that this is all too hard and too much work. And, in particular, this business of feeling and expressing your feelings is way too challenging.

Let's face it, some of us didn't grow up in environments where it was safe or wise to let it be known how we were feeling. And yet, as you saw in the last chapter, the more you become aware of your feelings and learn to open your Heart more fully, the more effective you'll likely be with Compassionate Self-Forgiveness.

Others have found the following information and suggestions to be very useful in gaining access to their emotional world and letting go of disturbing emotions. You'll also see and have the opportunity to use this very unique and useful tool in some unusual ways.

## Inner Pollution and the Process of Writing and Burning

These days, when a child is upset, they may be guided to spend a few minutes in a time-out room. The idea is to take a short period of quiet time to rebalance. There is an analogous thing that you, as an adult, can do that could support you in taking a restorative time-out when you find yourself experiencing emotional upset: the process of Free-Form Writing.*

The process of Free-Form Writing, more popularly known as Write and Burn among USM students, is a fabulous and freeing tool! It's simple, easy to do, and so supportive in letting go of "I'm upset because . . ." energy.

When you hold on to and stew in negative thoughts and feelings, it results in a kind of inner pollution in your consciousness. This inner pollution manifests in the form of disturbing emotions such as resentment, shame, guilt, irritation, frustration, anger, and hurt feelings, as well as negative thoughts and judgments associated with them. These unexpressed emotions and thoughts affect you, sometimes subtly and sometimes more obviously, contaminating and clouding your perception—to say nothing about how they adversely affect your stress levels and your health. It's for these reasons that we perceive "inner pollution" as an accurate description.

What can you do with the hidden tsunami of unexpressed disturbing thoughts and feelings? How can you let them go without having to experience the tidal wave of pent-up negative expressions and their inevitable negative consequences in your life, particularly in your relationships with yourself and others?

Write and Burn is just such a Practice. And the story of how it got its name is an interesting one!

One evening in class, a woman shared an extraordinary thing that had happened recently with her little boy. He had seen her doing Free-Form Writing and then burning what she had written. Being an inquiring sort of little guy, he asked her what on earth

---

* We learned Free-Form Writing from our Spiritual Teacher, John-Roger.

she was doing, then patiently listened to her explain both the process and her reasons for doing it.

One day after school, the first words out of his mouth as he returned home and took off his little backpack were, "Mommy, I need to Write and Burn."

We were all astonished *and* inspired by this child's amazing Awareness of what he needed to help himself rebalance after a challenging day at school and on the playground. He knew he needed to clean up his inner environment.

We took his example to Heart! After all, some days in the Earth School, the playground of life, can be very challenging. And as the little boy knew, one of the most Self-supporting things you can do as soon as you realize that you are upset is Write and Burn. By choosing to engage in Write and Burn, you are participating in the sacred process of letting go—clearing your consciousness of negativity and disturbance that block you from the realization of who you are: a Soul having a human experience.

Writing and Burning is truly a Practice through which you demonstrate Loyalty to your Soul. It involves powerful choices and intentions, including acknowledging that you're upset, Accepting that your "school is in session," letting go of "I'm upset because . . ." energy, and restoring yourself to your inherent Loving Essence. Thankfully, it neutralizes the trigger so you are no longer a walking "upset" looking for a good "because." It's a really good tool to have at your disposal whenever you feel yourself becoming disturbed.

### *Additional Options for Writing and Burning*

Writing and Burning is not only a great tool for expressing and letting go of emotional upset, it's also a tool of letting go of material residing in the deeper unconscious level of your psyche. The unconscious is a repository for material associated with your Spiritual Curriculum that, for one reason or another, your Soul is not yet ready to bring forward. And so, it simply sits there, surfacing like timed-release capsules when you are ready.

Like the mind and emotions, the unconscious is character-ized by duality. On the negative side, there may be material that is simply too frightening to consider at this stage of your Spiritual development. On the positive side, the unconscious is a reservoir of tremendous creativity. By tapping into your unconscious, the process of Writing and Burning can be a way of gaining access to your creative expression. You may discover some really amazing gifts and talents, which you're simply not yet ready to bring for-ward in your life.

It's important to understand that all this is simply a part of your Spiritual Curriculum and will be revealed in accordance with your Soul's timing. Have you ever had the experience of suddenly becoming aware of a feeling you've never felt before and finding yourself saying, "Wow, I didn't know that was in there"? If so, consider the possibility that you just revealed to yourself some-thing you were ready to allow to emerge from your unconscious-ness. This happens more often than most of us are aware.

One woman we knew, at first a budding playwright and then an accomplished *auteur dramatique,* as the French would say, some-times chose to do Writing and Burning before she would begin working on her current script. She found it a very helpful way of clearing the channel and priming the pump. Other students have reported similar experiences insofar as experiencing greater access, freedom, and inspiration in their creative expression.

Some students have chosen to do what we refer to as a 33-Day Process in which they participate in Writing and Burning each day. They determine a minimum amount of time—for example, 30 minutes for each session. They do this in service to clearing the unconscious, knowing that through Writing and Burning they may clear material such that it won't be necessary for them to consciously process it.

I (Mary) find that after Writing and Burning, I experience the Blessings of having taken a Spiritual Shower inside and out! So sacred and refreshing! I feel Shiny, Radiant, and Peaceful! Over the years, I've noticed Writing and Burning is one of the true power tools of Spiritual Psychology that supports Awakening.

┤ **THIS CHAPTER'S PRACTICE** ├

## *The 10 Steps for Writing and Burning*

This is a very supportive Practice you can use for releasing disturbing thoughts and feelings, tapping into your unconscious, and more. It's important that you read through the tips and steps outlined here before you begin. Remember not to use your journal for this purpose.

Step 1: We recommend you begin with a Centering meditation, Prayer, or Invocation such as the one that follows here:

"Source of Divine Love, of all that is, I ask for the Clearing . . . and that I be surrounded, protected, and filled with the Clear White Light of Spirit. I ask that only that which is for my Highest Good, and the Highest Good of all concerned, be brought forward. My intention is letting go of any negativity, disturbance, or imbalance that is present in service to restoring myself to the Peace, Joy, and Loving that are my true nature. So be it."

Step 2: Create a time and space in which you will not be disturbed by others, phones, e-mail, or other distractions. Some who practice Writing and Burning have found that putting a "Do Not Disturb" note on their door has been helpful in creating a sacred, private space. Once you begin, it's important not to be interrupted.

Step 3: You may want to light a candle before you begin as a way of signifying the sacredness of this letting-go process.

Step 4: Collect loose paper (not a journal) and a writing instrument. Writing and Burning is done by hand, using paper and a pen. It should not be on a computer or other digital device, as the energy released is not helpful for machinery. (We actually recommend you step away from your computer to do your Writing and Burning.)

Step 5: Write whatever is present. Sometimes people find that when the energy starts flowing fully, their writing becomes more like scribbling, and that's fine. It doesn't need to make sense, and it's okay to write in incomplete sentences with no concern for proper grammar, spelling, or punctuation. It's not uncommon to write something like: *"I saw my mom yesterday I really hate it when, STOP, This hurts . . . I'm so mad at . . ."*

Step 6: Do not attempt to censor or edit what is coming forward for you. The idea here is to go with the flow and express whatever comes forward in your consciousness.

Step 7: Write for a minimum of 10 minutes. You can write longer if you'd like, but it's best not to write for more than two hours in a single sitting. You can usually tell when you're complete, as your energy will tend to shift in the direction of neutrality—a more peaceful flow.

Step 8: Do *not* read over what you've written. You don't want to program it back into your consciousness. However, if something beautiful or inspirational comes through, flag or mark it so you can later copy it over on a separate piece of paper. Once you complete writing, go back and keep that piece only.

Step 9: If you notice that your Writing and Burning has judgment and upset emotional energy in it, you can write Compassionate Self-Forgiveness statements as an additional process and way of completing your writing.

Step 10: When you're finished, immediately burn or shred what you've written. Do not keep it. It's a final act of letting go. If you can't burn or shred it, tear it up into small pieces and dispose of it. You want to be sure that the writing is destroyed in such a way that your consciousness knows that no one else will be able to read it. Never share your writing with anyone else.

## INTENTION

I am practicing Writing and Burning in service to my Spiritual ecology, supporting myself in Awakening more fully into the Awareness of the Peace, Aliveness, Joy, Loving, Happiness, and Creativity of my Essential Nature.

CHAPTER 17

# THE WILD AND WONDERFUL WORLD OF CHOICES

*"Two roads diverged in a wood, and I—*
*I took the one less traveled by,*
*And that has made all the difference."*
— ROBERT FROST

Life is filled with choices, both little choices like vanilla or chocolate and big choices like career path and life partner. Inside the Context of Spiritual Psychology, the most significant choice you get to make is the choice to consciously engage in your Awakening or allow it to unfold in a more or less haphazard way while you sleep, a much more prolonged and painful approach. It's a choice to Accept and Cooperate with your life's Spiritual purpose. Indeed, it is *the* master choice of a lifetime. And it's a choice that you'll get to make over and over again as there are a cacophony of situations and circumstances that seductively lull you into drowsiness and, at times, deep slumber—sleepwalking through life—unaware of the multiple opportunities for Awakening being presented daily.

I (Mary) remember as a little girl, my family had just moved from a small lumber mill town in northern Wisconsin where my father, a modern-day circuit rider, ministered to memberships of four small churches in the surrounding area. We moved to a larger community on the shores of Lake Superior, where I would start kindergarten in the fall. Soon I was happily meeting other little girls in our new neighborhood, and in a short time we were engaged in a game of hopscotch. I was not doing particularly well and when my turn was complete, inside I heard a Voice say to me in the most Loving way: *"You're going to need to pay more attention here."*

Though I was five years old, that Voice got my attention, and it became my intention to "pay more attention here." That encounter with the small but powerful Voice within was formative—a kind of annunciation or introduction to my inner life. It was a true moment of Awakening—even at that early age—precipitating inside me the questions of, "Who am I?" "Why am I here?" and "What is my purpose?" The die was cast as I was already aware that there was more to my life than hopscotch, learning to read, or my father gently pushing me on the swing, which I loved as I felt a wonderful freedom in which I imagined I was flying!

For me, one of the Blessings of this experience was the Awareness that there was mystery and magic in life, and that by paying more attention, I would be given clues—clues that in retrospect I recognize as a road map to a life of Heart, Meaning, and Purpose. These clues would gently guide me in choosing to participate in my life as a process designed to foster conscious Awakening into the Awareness that I am a Divine Being having a human experience—in fact, a Divine Being *learning* to use my human experience for the Divine purpose of Awakening—and further, that my Inherent Nature is Wise and Loving, Compassionate and Creative, Resourceful and Resilient.

One big clue was delivered when I realized the power of choice in co-creating my life. At the time, I was living in a small university town in northern Idaho, less than a year after I had completed my doctoral studies and graduated. I was engaged in some housekeeping one Saturday morning when suddenly I had the Awareness, *"If it's going to be, it's up to me."* In that moment I realized my life was my responsibility and that I couldn't look to someone else to do it for me. And I realized that my choices would be one of the means through which I would construct the architecture of my life.

Choice is one of those wild and wonderful capacities that we as humans get to exercise. You are free to make choices in all areas of your life that result in greater Awareness of your Loving nature, or you can make choices that result in upset, disturbance, disappointment, frustration, loneliness, and the mental and emotional anguish of perceived separation from your inherently Loving Nature.

Recently Ron and I were having lunch with another couple, and the first words out of the wife's mouth were a story of victimization. I found myself sending her Loving thoughts while very aware that the story she was telling was one her ego had told thousands of times in the course of her life, although the details of her story varied from day to day. The choice she was making in telling the same story over and over perpetuated inner disturbance and unhappiness—yet she was completely unaware of it.

## *Outer and Inner Choices*

While you may never have thought about it in this way, you are constantly making choices both outwardly (in the world) and inwardly (your inner state, which is how you are going to be inside yourself, whether or not you do anything out in the world). Let's look at an example of how this works.

Consider any situation going on in your life that you'd like to be different. Perhaps it's a situation where you feel very much at the effect of other people or circumstances, such as with work or family. Or perhaps you would like to consider the inner and outer choices that you are making insofar as your Awakening is concerned. While practicing Seeing the Loving Essence and Heart-Centered Listening with yourself, consider the following questions:

(1) Are there any inner or outer choices you see yourself making that tend to perpetuate this situation?

*Examples of outer choices* include those pertaining to different *actions* you could take such as what job to accept, whether to attend an event, calling friends/family, making a purchase, going out with someone, furthering your education, or taking a trip.

*Examples of inner choices* include those pertaining to choosing your *attitude*—is it blaming/judgmental or is it Accepting/Compassionate/Loving—toward yourself, someone else, or a situation; or choosing the nature and direction of your inner self-talk.

(2) Are there any other choices (inner and/or outer) you *might* make that would produce different results?

(The key here is in knowing you don't have to do anything differently. You're simply checking whether you can see any alternatives. You're not committing to doing anything.)

The outer choices you make are important, and even more important are the attitudinal, inner choices. One of the most powerful inner choices we know that supports Awakening is consciously choosing to reside in my Loving—to live my days in Loving Kindness with an Open Heart to the best of my ability. That choice is a game changer, and you'll likely find it fosters the experience of the Sweetness of your Being as your Loving Essence naturally flows into all you do and to everyone you meet.

As one of the Spiritual Psychology Principles states: "How you relate to an issue *is* the issue; or, how you relate with yourself while you go through an issue *is* the issue." You can translate that to: "How you relate with yourself as you go through your day is the opportunity!" After all, you are a Soul having a human experience. You are worthy of your own Loving Kindness and nurturance. You have choices! Radiating and sharing your Loving is choosing the Power of Love, a state of Authentic Empowerment. And it's a hallmark of your Awakening.

## Choosing Alignment with
## Your Authentic Self, Your Soul

If you're interested in discovering your private elevator up in terms of your Spiritual Awakening, consider the question, "What does it mean experientially for me to be loyal to my Authentic Self?" Exploring this question can support you in greater Awareness of your choices and, more specifically, Awareness of the choices that are an expression of loyalty to your Authentic Self.

Take a few moments in the Silence and attune to your Loving. Then inwardly ask, "What does it mean experientially for me to be loyal to my Authentic Self, to my Soul?" Now engage in Heart-Centered Listening in the Silence.

When you're ready, respond in your journal five or more times to the following stem sentence: "One way I can be loyal to my Authentic Self, to my Soul, is . . ." Then take a few minutes to consider choices that may foster the experiences you wrote.

Here are a few responses that came forward for Mary:

- *Spending time in deep listening in the Silence.*

- *Relaxing . . . and simply being.*

- *Letting go of any preconceived agendas about who I am and what I need to do.*

- *Recognizing that I am the Voice of Love and allowing myself to express that.*

- *More fully accepting my love of Beauty (in people, art, the environment, etc.).*

- *Enjoying open, unstructured time in my schedule.*

- *Asking inwardly, "What would my Soul love me to do?"*

- *Being devoted with my Spiritual practice.*

- *Knowing I am the Presence of Love and living into that Awareness.*

- *Surrendering my life to God.*

If you'd like to take this inquiry further, respond five or more times to this second stem sentence: "I feel most loyal to my Authentic Self, to my Soul, when I . . ." Once again, take a few minutes afterward to consider choices that may foster the experiences you wrote.

Here are a few of Mary's responses:

- *Experience the Presence of Love.*

- *Experience myself as on purpose in my life.*

- *Experience the Joy of being of service to others.*

- *Pay attention to and honor the Still, Small Voice within and make Self-Honoring choices.*

- *When I feel fully used.*

- *Am surrendering to Love and being used as God's pencil.*

- *Am aware of the Divine Perfection of my life.*

Living in the Awareness that you *can* make choices that support you in your Awakening is what's important. This does not entail moving to an ashram, although some may choose that path; and it certainly doesn't mean depriving yourself of what you enjoy in life. It's not about deprivation and austerity; it's about Love, Joy, Aliveness, Fulfillment, Meaning, and Purpose—and Paying Attention!

Perhaps most essentially, it means conducting your life inside the Awareness that you are a Divine Being having a human experience; that your Essential Nature, and that of everyone else, is Loving; and that you can learn to discern and make choices that support you in experiencing a wonderful and fulfilling life on both the Goal Line and Soul Line as you Awaken. It's choosing to live your life to the best of your ability as the Presence of Love, knowing this truly is "the road less traveled."

We encourage you in noticing the choices you are making and whether these are in harmony with the Wisdom of your Heart and your intended outcomes. Your choices are one of the primary ways you are architecting your life. One of the Spiritual Psychology Principle states: "You create your future by how you respond to your experiences now." As Eleanor Roosevelt said: "In the long run, we shape our lives and we shape ourselves. The process never ends until we die. And the choices we make are ultimately our own responsibility."

Let yourself be one about whom it is said, "You chose wisely!"

## THIS CHAPTER'S PRACTICES

In this chapter, we've presented two possible Practices or experiments that can assist you in exploring the dimension of choice as you participate in them.

### *Observing Both Your Inner and Outer Choices*

This first Practice involves noticing the choices you're making—both inner and outer. Inwardly, you really do choose your attitude toward how you relate with yourself, others, and the situations and circumstances in your life. Will it be judging or Accepting, criticizing or prizing?

We invite you to practice Seeing the Loving Essence and Heart-Centered Listening with yourself as you journal about a situation in your life while reflecting on the following two questions:

- Are there any inner or outer choices you see yourself making that tend to perpetuate this situation?

- Are there any other choices (inner and/or outer) you *might* make which would produce different results?

Simply write your answers down as they come to you so that you can reflect upon them whenever you'd like. Remember, the key here is in knowing you don't *have* to do anything differently. You're simply looking to see if you can see any alternatives. You're not committing to doing anything.

### Ways I Can Be Loyal to My Authentic Self— to My Soul

Writing in your journal, respond five or more times to the following stem sentence: *One way I can be loyal to my Authentic Self— to my Soul—right now is . . .*

Reflect on your responses. Perhaps they are signposts revealing some choices for you to reflect upon and consider.

If you'd like to take this inquiry further, respond five or more times to this stem sentence: *I feel most loyal to my Authentic Self—to my Soul—when I . . .*

---

## INTENTION

I am slooowing down and consciously choosing my responses
to what life brings me. I am relating with myself, and others,
in more Accepting, Kind, and Openhearted ways.
I am embodying Loyalty to my Soul.

---

# CHAPTER 18

# AWAKENING WHILE SLEEPING

*"Awakening is not a thing. It is not a goal, not a concept.*
*It is not something to be attained. It is a metamorphosis.*
*If the caterpillar thinks about the butterfly it is to become,*
*saying 'And then I shall have wings and antennae,' there will*
*never be a butterfly. The caterpillar must accept its own*
*disappearance in its transformation. When the marvelous*
*butterfly takes wing, nothing of the caterpillar remains."*

— ALEJANDRO JODOROWSKY

Now that you've opened up the dimension of choices, we'd love to share with you several options and tools that we have found to be very useful in living more of an Awakened life. For example, while it may seem odd, sleep time is just such an opportunity for utilizing one of the tools.

You may be wondering how you can foster a good night's sleep, given the demands of your life, your concerns and challenges, and whatever patterns you're currently experiencing regarding your sleep or lack thereof. I (Ron) learned one method from Spiritual Master Swami Satchidananda, who was often asked about how he managed to fall asleep at night given all his responsibilities. While attending a lecture of his many years ago, I heard him share that when he lay down at the end of his day and closed his eyes, he prayed, "Lord God, I've done all I can do today. If you'd like me to do any more tomorrow, please wake me in the morning." What sage advice from a sage!

If you're anything like me (Mary), you probably grew up thinking of sleep as a time for resting your body so that you can be prepared for tomorrow. Although from as early as I remember I had an active dream life, it was a while before I consciously considered the possibility that my time sleeping could also be prime time for communing with Spirit and receiving guidance.

Having dealt with sleep issues at various times throughout my life, developing practices that foster replenishing sleep is something I'm very aware of and have been engaged with for many years. What a relief to find that as I've become more and more involved in Spiritual Awakening, I've also learned several processes that have assisted me greatly in not only getting a higher quality of rest, but also in utilizing my sleep time as a wonderful opportunity for bypassing the egocentricities of my mind and receiving guidance from a deeper Source. As paradoxical as it may seem, I became aware of my sleeping as a process that I could utilize in service to my Spiritual Awakening.

In particular, I've developed several practices that have been, and continue to be, extremely successful for me. One that I've found to be very helpful is developing a well-established sleep ritual that I use every evening as part of preparing to go to sleep. It has three distinct parts. The first is Preparing Your Body and Consciousness for Sleep. The second is a process of Setting Bedtime Intentions, and the third is asking for guidance on any question using the process of Asking Dream Incubation Questions.

Let's begin with the first process.

### *Preparing Your Body and Consciousness for Sleep*

One of the biggest keys to sleeping well is slooowing down, especially during the period before settling down to go to sleep. Here's the process I (Mary) use:

- I discontinue using all electronic devices an hour before bed.

- I run a hot bath and take a nice long soak in almost total darkness as a way of relaxing my body and letting go of the day. During this time, I clear my consciousness of any judgments or upsets I may be experiencing through a process of letting them go by applying Loving to them. I do this primarily through the process of Compassionate Self-Forgiveness for judgments of myself, others, the world, etc., that I may have placed during the day; and through Loving inner conversation with any part inside that may be upset. I find these two ways of being with myself clear my energy, restore greater balance, and bring a sense of completion to whatever I've experienced that day—a process I find essential to clearing my mind in preparation for restful sleep.

- I then do my teeth and skin-care regimens.

- I wear a cozy cashmere robe and soft slippers that I experience as comforting and nurturing.

- When I turn down the bed, I notice a little pillow I keep on the bed, which has an image of an angel on it. Its presence signals me that it's time to sleep.

- Just before I get into bed, I wind my music box, which plays a favorite piece of music that I have loved since I was a child. (I even have a miniature music box that I take with me when I travel.) I then get into bed and listen to it play "Silent Night." There's something about hearing the beautiful sounds and familiar music that evokes a sense of Peace. And, of course, the music, though wordless, conveys to me, "Sleep in heavenly peace . . . sleep in heavenly peace."

- This is followed by a Practice Ron and I have had for many years that involves sharing three rounds of appreciations about ourselves and each other as a way of completing the day. We do this without fail. It's a way of consciously bringing ourselves in the Loving before we go to sleep.

- I then cover my eyes with a weighted eye pillow, lightly scented with lavender.

Of course, what I do is not a prescription for what *you* should do. Mine is tailor-made for me, and I share it here simply to give you some ideas. Create your own routine for slooowing down and sending a clear signal to both your body and your consciousness that it's time to wind down, let go of the day, and get ready for some beautiful quiet time cradled in the arms of Spirit's Love.

### Setting Bedtime Intentions

The second process I refer to as Setting Bedtime Intentions, and I enter into it with an attitude of Gratitude wonderfully expressed in this popular prayer by Ralph Waldo Emerson:

*For each new morning with its light,*
*For rest and shelter of the night,*
*For health and food, for love and friends,*
*For everything Thy goodness sends.*

Essentially, Bedtime Intentions are a way of asking for Spirit's assistance, trusting that Spirit has your best interests (Highest Good) at Heart, and directly inviting Spirit to participate in the Awakening of your consciousness and in the matters of your daily life. It's another way of aligning yourself to participate consciously in the co-creative process of living your life.

When expressed from a sincere and Grateful Heart, Bedtime Intentions become a form of Prayer, a way of communicating your Gratitude, Heartfelt intentions, and requests for assistance to the Divine. I sometimes refer to Bedtime Intentions as the lazy person's way to Enlightenment!

Well, you ask, what if I don't believe in God, or Spirit, or the Divine? As strange as it may seem, belief is not a requirement in order to participate in the process. With the attitude of the Spiritual Scientist, you can conduct an experiment and experientially determine for yourself the results.

Assuming you're ready to conduct the experiment, here are the steps:

## The Process of Setting Bedtime Intentions

Step 1: Find a comfortable position where you can move into a state of relaxed attention. Some people like to lie down while others prefer to sit on the edge of their bed with their feet on the floor and their back straight. There's no right way, only the way that works for you. You can try both to determine which seems to work best.

Step 2: Clarify the intention or intentions you'd like to place into Spirit (or whatever word or phrase works for you, such as Great Heart of the Universe, Higher Power, Light of Living Love, etc.). Some people like to write their Bedtime Intentions as a way of supporting them in specificity and clarity.

Step 3: Begin your intentions by Centering yourself within your Heart, within the Loving that is the Essence of who you are.

Step 4: Offer a simple Heartfelt prayer: "Father Mother God, I call myself forward into your Light and Loving, asking to be cleared through the Holy Spirit and to be filled, surrounded, and protected with the Clear White Light of Living Love. I ask that I be flooded with Loving."

(**Note:** This step is asking that any negative energy you may have picked up during the day be cleared from your energy field. It is also a way of asking for Spiritual protection while you sleep.)

Step 5: Ask for only that which is for your Highest Good to be brought forward.

Step 6: State your intentions. You can state them out loud or in the Silence of your own Heart.

Step 7: Release your intentions into the Light of Spirit, the Light of Living Love.

Step 8: Share Gratitude with Spirit for all the Blessings of the day and all you have experienced and learned.

Step 9: Go to sleep knowing that your intentions have been heard by Spirit.

That's all there is to it. Once you get the hang of it—which, of course, is a direct result of nightly practice—you'll find that the process takes but a few minutes. You can also use this time to place people and situations in your life into the Light for the Highest Good.

One of my favorite quotes by Kahlil Gibran, a Lebanese-American poet, is from his well-known work *The Prophet*. In the chapter "On Love," he writes: "To wake at dawn with a winged heart and give thanks for another day of Loving."

A restful night's sleep truly refreshes the body and Spirit, and I arise with a sense of well-being and readiness to give thanks for another day of Loving.

## Examples of Bedtime Intentions

- I ask that whatever can be lifted and cleared during the sleep state be done under Grace and for the Highest Good of all concerned.

- Please show me my next steps regarding [a relationship, a specific project, a health situation, a creative endeavor, etc.] in a way that I can recognize and understand for the Highest Good.

- I ask that You assist me in releasing the misunderstandings, misinterpretations, and misidentifications that have held me into the pattern of [over-responsibility, approval seeking, self-judgment, unworthiness, emotional reactivity, etc.].

- Given my gifts, experience, education, and abilities, please show me how I can be of greatest service.

- Please assist me in experientially knowing that I am the Loving, that I am a Divine Being having a human experience.


## *Asking Dream Incubation Questions: A Tool for Awakening*

The third process I work with is called Asking Dream Incubation Questions, and it is not necessarily a tool I utilize every night. Rather, I utilize this tool when I have questions about which I'm seeking Spiritual Guidance. I find it works best to formulate my actual questions before I begin my physical bedtime ritual so that I can bring my full consciousness to bear on the process of clarifying my question. As Carl Jung said, "The dream is a little hidden door in the innermost and most secret recesses of the soul."

Dream Incubation is a process of preparing the consciousness to receive a guidance dream; it is an extension of Setting Bedtime Intentions. This process has been practiced for centuries, and its origins can be traced to ancient Greece, where people would go to a Healing temple to dream in order to receive guidance (including a diagnosis and treatment for their health issues).

Dream Incubation Questions are a vehicle through which anyone with clarity of intention and practice can gain direct access to Spiritual Wisdom, Guidance, and Inner Knowing. In other words, you can foster the experience of your own Awakening through this Practice. As Synesius of Cyrene, a Greek bishop living around the year A.D. 400, is reported to have said, "Dreams offer themselves to all. They are oracles, always ready to serve as our silent and infallible counselors."

The purpose of using the Dream Incubation process is to assist in:

- Identifying an area in which you would like to receive guidance.

- Clarifying the question you would like answered.

- Clarifying a protocol that maximizes the possibility of remembering your dream.

The following questions are designed to help you clarify and refine your Dream Incubation Question:

- In what area of your life would you like to receive guidance regarding a particular situation, relationship, concern, difficulty, decision, or next step?

- What specifically do you want to know?

- Being completely honest with yourself, are there any benefits, advantages, or payoffs that you get from *not* receiving guidance in this area? If so, what are they?

- What information have you gathered so far concerning this area? Or, what pieces of the puzzle do you have knowledge of at this point?

- What question do you want answered? Formulate your question carefully and precisely. Write a short, specific sleep suggestion that you can use tonight— a brief statement of the question that you can focus on as you drift off to sleep.

- Place your Dream Incubation Question into the Light and ask for Spirit's assistance for the Highest Good. Since the language of dreams is metaphorical and symbolic, I suggest that you ask that the answer to your question be given in a way that you can recognize and understand.

Maintain a dream journal, separate from your regular journal, in which you write your responses to these questions as well as record your dreams. Keep it beside your bed within easy reach. This will support you in recording any dreams you remember as soon as you awaken, which is when you're most likely to recall them.

Then, just prior to settling down for a long winter's nap, set an intention to remember your dreams. In an authentic and Heart-felt manner, ask your question directly to Spirit, asking only that which is for your Highest Good be brought forward. This helps release attachment and creates openness to receiving Spirit's guidance. Then go to sleep.

When you awaken (and this is very important), remain totally still—do not move your body. This allows you greater access to your dream—better dream recall. Once you have your dream secure in your awareness, your first movement should be to get your pen and dream journal, and begin writing any dreams or parts of dreams that you recall.

Sometimes you'll be able to recall a dream the very first night that you ask your Dream Incubation Question. Sometimes you may find that you need to ask your question for several nights. I encourage you to be patient and let go of any pressure or attachment to receiving a dream.

One of the best ways to clarify the meaning and message of your dreams is to give various objects or people in the dream a voice. I encourage you to write not only the dream, but then to also write what the objects or people say when you give them a voice. Keeping a dream journal is a tremendous tool for discovering the metaphorical messages of your dreams and also for noticing the qualitative difference in dreams that you have.

### Ron's Dream Incubation Question and Dream

A great example of asking a Dream Incubation Question and having a subsequent meaningful dream occurred when I (Ron) utilized the process of Dream Incubation and asked a question pertaining to my future.

Every now and then, I've had a particularly incisive dream, like the time many years ago when I'd been pondering the question, "What would life be like if I dared live more fully from within the perspective of the Spiritual Context?" I then had the following dream.

*I'm driving at normal speed along a two-lane country road in New Mexico, and all of a sudden my car veers off the road and onto the desert floor. I attempt to gain control, since there are many large cactus plants where I'm driving and I need to avoid them. I'm aware that the car is picking up speed, so I step on the brake. The pedal goes down to the floor—no brakes—and the car is going faster and faster. I'm steering like mad around the cactus plants, and then the steering mechanism becomes dysfunctional. The car is picking up speed and I have no way of steering it. And then I notice that regardless of what I do, the car is steering itself just fine regardless of how fast it's going. I take a deep breath, relax, and enjoy the ride.*

The metaphorical message of this dream for me was about letting go of the illusion of control and moving into learning to live a more surrendered life in harmony with Spirit's plan for me.

### Mary's Dream Incubation Question and Dream

Some time ago, I (Mary) was thinking about restructuring my role in my work at the University. It seemed to me I had too many roles and responsibilities, and that more of my time was involved with activities of administrative maintenance, which was not my preference nor in harmony with my deepest Heartfelt yearnings. I had scheduled a meeting to discuss this with a trusted advisor so that together we could review my job description with any eye toward a radical pruning. I was leaning toward redefining my work as facilitating classes and writing books, developing new courses (both in person and online), and working with a few coaching or counseling clients. I had been placing my question regarding this change into the Light and asking for Spirit's guidance about this change. About a week before the meeting, I had the following dream.

*I'm moving from my office at the University, and someone is escorting me to my new office. When we arrive and open the door, I see a windowless room decorated entirely in white; it seems rather stark and bare. It's long, narrow, and rather small. There isn't even room for my couch. I immediately say, "This is a mistake. I can't work in here."*

*I immediately leave that office with my escort and walk down the corridor to return to my former office. When we arrive, the room is the same as my current (real) office with its beautiful floor-to-ceiling windows, yet the space has been transformed, with everything being a radiant white. While the other office had also been entirely white, in contrast this room is filled with luminous Light.*

*My escort points out the three white valances near the top of the window, indicating that they are samples from which I can select. Two are rather plain—adequate enough. The third is beautiful, simple yet elegant, with a kind of feminine Grace. I immediately choose it and experience a sense of Joy and Peace, feeling very at Home.*

The message of this dream was clear to me. It was important that I not assign myself a new role that would be too narrow or restrictive for myself. I needed to retain my leadership and oversight roles; however, I was free to change the way I was accomplishing them. I could utilize other resources to facilitate my goals. Any angst, concern, or internal pressure regarding a need to make a change had completely dissolved.

When I went to my meeting with my trusted advisor, I was in a place of clarity and knowing that all was well; no outer change was to be made. An inner transformation had taken place, changing my relationship to my work inside of me.

This experience was a powerful reminder for me of the value of practicing Heart-Centered Listening Within Yourself. Know that no Heartfelt question to Spirit goes unanswered. All we need do is ask and then open to receive the Blessings that already are.

## THIS CHAPTER'S PRACTICES

There are three Practices included in this chapter you can utilize in service to restful sleep and to Awakening. We recommend cultivating them in sequence.

### Preparing Your Body and Your Consciousness for Sleep

Develop your own personalized process for Preparing Your Body and Your Consciousness for Sleep. Review the process included in this chapter to spark your own ideas and write them in your journal.

### Setting Bedtime Intentions

Conduct your own experiments utilizing the nine steps for Setting Bedtime Intentions. Write your experiences in your journal.

### Asking Dream Incubation Questions

Clarify an area in which you'd like to ask a Dream Incubation Question and follow the six steps outlined in this chapter. Record your questions and your dreams in your journal.

## INTENTION

I am Setting Bedtime Intentions and Asking Dream Incubation Questions. I am opening my Spiritual eyes, lifting the veil of forgetfulness as I am becoming Awake—Remembering Who I Am. I am cultivating my Inner Knowing, trusting Spirit's Guidance—discovering the magic of Awakening while sleeping.

# CHAPTER 19

# LIVING INTO AN AWAKENED LIFE: EXPERIENCING JOY THROUGH SERVICE

*"The day will come when, after harnessing the winds, the tides and gravitation, we shall harness for God the energies of love. And on that day, for the second time in the history of the world, man will have discovered fire."*

— TEILHARD DE CHARDIN

In the previous chapters, we shared many tools we have found useful in living a more Awakened life. The one we'll be working with in this chapter is unusual in that it can function both as a tool of Awakening and also as an *expression* of living an Awakened life. We're sure you'll recognize it. You may already be involved in some form of it. It's called *service*.

Service is the natural impulse of the Soul. It evokes the most splendid and exquisite sentiments in the Heart, bringing forward Generosity of Spirit and a sense of Meaning, Purpose, and Fulfillment that is beyond compare. Participating in service is indeed one of the ways you can Awaken more fully into the Awareness of the Love and Joy that you are—and reside there.

## The Value of Service

Some years ago, I (Mary) had gradually become increasingly involved in supporting my aging parents. They were in their early nineties and still living in their large two-story home on a spacious corner lot in a small rural Midwestern community. Their home was filled to overflowing with a lifetime accumulation of "things" representing collections of many treasured memories and cherished experiences. Needless to say, their home and property, never mind their belongings, required considerable maintenance. Although they both were physically vital and in possession of their mental faculties, it was too much for them to maintain and the volume had become overwhelming for them.

I, along with my sisters and brother, became concerned for their health and safety. At some point along the way, collecting had become hoarding, and massive clutter creep had occurred. My siblings expressed their concern to our parents, who thanked them yet remained intractable in their attachment to their "things." One sibling threatened to report my parents to a county health agency if they didn't do something about "the mess," since much of it was accumulated paper, which represented a growing fire hazard.

It was at that point that I chose to become more involved. I couldn't bear the thought of my parents having to deal with the intervention of an outside agency, as I knew it would be distressing to them. A combination of Love and responsibility was moving inside of me. And, in all honesty, I must admit that the condition of their home deeply offended my sense of aesthetics! (Yes, I did work my process of Forgiving my judgments and opening my Heart to a place of Acceptance and Compassion, as I recognize that I have an inherited genetic propensity that seems to draw paper to me like iron filings are drawn to a magnet.)

It wasn't long before Ron and I were on a plane from California on Mission: Family Intervention. We held the intention to have a respectful conversation with my mom and dad such that they would hopefully agree we could restore their home to a level of cleanliness and order that would simplify things, be healthier for them, and defuse the concerns of other family members.

Thank God that Ron and I made this trip together, as he was masterful in communicating our concerns, our respect for them and their home, and an appreciation on our part for their attachment to their "things." Thank God for the Soul-Centered skills of Seeing the Loving Essence, Heart-Centered Listening, Perception Checking, and Acceptance, which reigned in all their simple glory. My mom and dad agreed to the proposed cleaning and decluttering, and the work began.

For six days, we sorted, scrubbed, and did whatever was needed in service to my parents and their well-being. We began each day with an early morning trip to a delightful local coffee shop and bookstore, fortifying ourselves with lattes, biscotti, and poetic inspiration. Midafternoons, we went to the local sweet shop for some *very* indulgent ice cream bars, convincing ourselves that they were *necessary* to keep up our strength. Thank goodness we were very physically active, so we weren't packing on the weight we were releasing in excess paper. When we were done, we had removed more than 300 large garbage bags filled with paper and probably 50 cartons of old magazines—to say nothing about all the reorganizing.

When we got on the plane to return to California and wearily collapsed into our very comfortable seats, the feeling of Joy we experienced was indescribable! I assure you, it didn't have anything to do with the seats. We had spent a week physically working much harder than we were accustomed to. And yet, here we were, overflowing with Joy and experiencing deep Fulfillment and even Gratitude for the experience. We were experiencing the Joy of service. We were truly in an expanded and elevated state of consciousness that continued for some time.

Now why might that be? As Rabindranath Tagore said, "I slept and dreamt that life was joy. I awoke and saw that life was service. I acted and behold, service was joy." Consider that when you are truly being of service, and by that we mean that you have no ulterior motive other than being of service, you are residing within your Authentic Self. In fact, it's impossible not to. Why? You can only share what you have, so to share Loving you are *in* Loving. And the more time you can reside in that state, the more you are experiencing the nature of what a fully Awakened Being experiences. In psychological terms, you are positively reinforcing the process of Awakening.

The entire experience was a teaching about the value of service and its contribution to Awakening. Service, as we see it, is a vehicle for transformation and experiencing the Unconditional Love and Joy of your Authentic Self. As George Bernard Shaw wrote, "This is the true joy in life, the being used for a purpose recognized by yourself as a mighty one . . . the being a force of Nature instead of a feverish selfish little clod of ailments and grievances complaining that the world will not devote itself to making you happy."

We encourage you to consider committing to and participating in some kind of service project of your choosing as one of your experiments in Awakening. Select whatever has resonance for you. Perhaps it's going to a military base and participating in a holiday party for wounded veterans, or visiting those in a nursing home in your community, who will be strangers to you only at the beginning. Perhaps you'll be volunteering as a teacher's aide in a classroom or by holding newborns in a hospital nursery. Perhaps your service project will have to do with feeding baby birds at a wildlife center or cleaning up a beach or bay. The opportunities are infinite. They are only awaiting your answering the Calling of your Heart to be of service.

## Experiencing the Joy of Service through Random Acts of Kindness

We invite you to recall a moment when your Heart was touched and your response was an outpouring of your Loving and Caring that manifested in service, perhaps a small random act of kindness. Or perhaps you can recall a time when someone was of service to you, and how touched and Grateful you were. William Wordsworth said it well: "Small service is true service while it lasts: / [. . .] / The Daisy, by the shadow that it casts, / Protects the lingering dew-drop from the Sun."

A couple of years ago, we were spending a few days in Santa Fe, New Mexico, participating in a three-day continuing-education seminar. We like to visit Santa Fe each October to take in the majesty of the mountains and the glory of the golden aspens. It also happily reminds us of the years during which we met, taught, and lived in New Mexico. During the course of the seminar, we were in the habit of making an early-morning run to the local coffeehouse to pick up chai lattes before class, which began promptly at 8 A.M.

One morning while I (Mary) was waiting in line to order, I noticed the young man ahead of me carefully counting out his coins. It was soon apparent that he was short the amount for his order. I experienced a genuine sweetness about him, and I said to the barista, "Please add his charges to mine." The words were barely out of my mouth when my Heart opened and my eyes moistened. His and my eyes met. It was truly a Soul Moment—a moment of Love seeing into Love, of God seeing into God. The Blessing I received was an instantaneous overflowing of Divine Love, an experience transcending words.

I do not know his name or story, and yet, when I recall the experience, my Heart is touched and I send him Blessings of Light and Loving for his Highest Good, trusting that they are indeed received. Did you know you receive a Blessing of Love every time you share one? In fact, it's impossible not to.

What a thing—to Bless . . . and to be Blessed.

Know that the value of service is not measured in the bigness or grandness of what you do. It's in the quality of Love that you share—your wholeheartedness.

For your further inspiration, we're sharing one of our favorite quotes by Daphne Rose Kingma:

> Random acts of kindness are those little sweet or grand lovely things we do for no reason except that, momentarily, the best of our humanity has sprung, exquisitely, into full bloom.
>
> When you spontaneously give an old woman the bouquet of red carnations you had meant to take home to your own dinner

table, when you give your lunch to the guitar-playing beggar who makes music at the corner between your two subway stops, when you anonymously put coins in someone else's parking meter because you see the red "Expired" medallion signaling to a meter maid—you are doing not what life requires of you, but what the best of your human soul invites you to do.

## Deepening in Service through Writing and Offering a Service Prayer

One of the things we've found very useful over the years is for each of us to have a Service Prayer. This prayer is a way of deepening in the consciousness of service and letting Spirit know that it's our intention to be of service. It's a lovely Practice to review your Service Prayer each morning as a way of setting the tone and direction for your day, or before you participate in the focus of your service.

Here is a simple Service Prayer that I (Mary) offer before I begin a class or a coaching session with someone:

"Dear Father Mother God, I ask that I be cleared, filled, surrounded, and protected with the Light of Living Love. I ask that only that which is for the Highest Good be brought forward, keeping in mind our unique destinies on this planet. I ask that I be used as a conduit of your Love, your Light and Sound, your Healing Grace—an instrument of your Peace and Presence. My intention is Loving service. I ask that thy will be done. For this opportunity and all the Blessings of my life, I give Gratitude. So be it."

What is it that makes the experience of service so compelling, even addictive? At USM, the tradition of service is integral to the fabric of the University. Year after year, hundreds of graduates of the program participate in volunteer service—assisting with the logistical support for the classes, or reading and responding to students' home assignments under the supervision of faculty. It's the Joy that comes from doing with Love whatever needs to be done with no thought of what you'll receive in return. We refer to it as a Culture of Giving.

Service is actually a fast track to Awakening. Very often some of what you may experience as restrictions, limitations, and disturbances falls away—and what is left is the Beauty of the Soul.

One woman who took the three years of our classes in Spiritual Psychology had a radical and profound transformation. During the third year, her dour disposition evaporated, and she became a Light Beam of Effervescent Cheerfulness and Joy. When asked about it, she said, "I've learned that Loving is my service."

## THIS CHAPTER'S PRACTICES

For this chapter, once again we are including three Practices. And, of course, as the budding Spiritual Scientist that you are, you can participate in one, none, or all of these to see how any of them work for you.

### *Participate in Small Acts of Service*

We invite you to set your intention to be of service. Consider committing to doing a minimum of one random act of kindness each day for at least the next two weeks. It could be as simple as sending someone Blessings of Love for their Highest Good. (And remember that you receive a Blessing of Love for every one you share.) With your clear intention to be of service, you may be pleasantly surprised by the serendipitous opportunities your life brings you.

Briefly write in your journal about each of your random acts of kindness, describing: (1) the situation, (2) what you did as your random act of kindness, and (3) what you experienced.

### *Participate in a Larger Service Project*

Select a short- or long-term service project to which you're drawn. Participate in it with the intention of residing in the service consciousness and experiencing the Unconditional Loving and Joy of your Authentic Self.

Write your experiences in your journal each time you serve. Notice any shifts in consciousness that occur, and any overflow or blessing that takes place in your everyday life.

### *Write a Service Prayer*

Write a Service Prayer and read it each morning as a way of setting your intention to be of service. (You can review the prayer we offer in this chapter for ideas.) Write in your journal your reflections about how you experience your day when you approach it from the service consciousness.

## INTENTION

I am cultivating the consciousness of Loving Service,
bringing Blessings of Light and Loving wherever I go,
for in so doing, I know that I, too, am Blessed.
I am Awakening into the Joy of Service.

# CHAPTER 20

# SINGING YOUR SOUL'S SONG

*"I am a hole in the flute that the Christ's breath moves through—
Listen to this music."*

— HAFIZ

Service is not only a powerful way of living into an Awakened life but also one of the ways many people experience a greater sense of Meaning, Fulfillment, and Purpose.

Perhaps you've been pondering your own purpose for some time—wondering, "How can I recognize and *know* my purpose, let alone Accept and live into it? How do I get from where I am now to living a more fulfilling Soul-Centered Life?" We have what we believe you'll find a very empowering response: *by Accepting and daring to live more fully into the experience of your Divinity.*

You may be saying to yourself, "That doesn't sound very practical . . . I need to earn a living. And if I did dare to Accept and live more fully into the experience of my Divinity, what on earth would that look like? I have no idea what that means or how to do it."

Believe it or not, the answers could very well be closer than you imagine. Consider the following possibility, simultaneously radical and simple: *You can discover your purpose by owning both the qualities and gifts inherent within your Authentic Self and taking actions you perceive a Divinely inspired person would take.* In this way, you open yourself to *experiencing* greater levels of Purpose, Meaning, and Fulfillment.

One of my (Mary's) favorite affirmations came forward many years ago: "I am Accepting and Expressing the Loving Heart that I am." It's short, and saying it either out loud or in the Silence of my Heart immediately has the effect of bringing me into Loving Resonance with my Authentic Self. It supports me in standing up more fully in my Essential Nature and sharing the Goodness, the Godness, the Unconditional Loving of who—or more accurately, what—I am.

Here's an approach you can use to support yourself in Accepting and daring to live more fully in the *experience* of your Divinity. Try it out and see what you experience.

## *Who Inspires You?*

This Practice is an opportunity to identify a person who inspires you and to begin acknowledging, owning, and Accepting the wondrous capacities they are reflecting to you. It may be someone you know, a famous person you've never met, or a historical figure who's no longer alive. Know that the person you choose is a Divine Being whose unique expression of their Soul Essence is mirroring the Majesty of your Soul, resonating in harmony with your God-given gifts.

Here, we include an example of one person's response to this Practice.

1. Who is the person? What do they represent to you?
*Mahatma Gandhi. For me he is the embodiment of a great Soul who became the Presence of Peace and led from that consciousness.*

2. What is it about them that inspires you? Is it a quality, something about their character, something they contributed or accomplished?
*His Strength of Heart and his way of Being—Peaceful, filled with Love, Respect, Purpose, Service, and Wisdom.*

3. What is the experience that is evoked inside of you when you think of this person?

*I went into a vast place of Silence inside in which I'm experiencing Awe, Reverence, and Respect.*

4. If you give that experience a voice, what would it say? (As a way of owning and accepting the experience and the qualities, say the statements out loud, beginning with "I am.")

*I am experiencing Strength of Heart, steadfastly sharing the Peaceful Presence that I am. I am Reverence. I am Respect. I am Wisdom. I am Love. I am Peace.*

5. Can you think of any ways in which you can take action that would be a living demonstration of your expressing these qualities? What are they?

*I can respond more Peacefully with my partner, my children, my co-workers, and with my parents. I can also send Loving and Blessings of Peace to all people, life forms, conditions, situations, and countries across the planet for the Highest Good of all Concerned.*

6. Actually express out loud, or write down, a description of yourself taking these steps in the present. (Note that you are not committing to actually doing anything beyond this process.)

*Each morning, I am bringing forward the Strength of my Heart and stating my intention of holding a Peaceful Presence with my partner, my children, my co-workers, and with my parents. Each morning, I am sending Blessings of Loving and Peace to all people, life forms, conditions, situations, and countries across the planet for the Highest Good of all Concerned.*

You may be getting a sense that this beautiful process of owning your Inherent Goodness and Greatness is actually relatively simple. However, you're probably aware through your own experience that it's also not that easy. Self-doubt and self-judgment get in the way because of your belief in the ego's story—a story of misidentification of your self as unworthy.

In this world, it's very easy to be seduced by your ego and to misidentify with feelings of unworthiness. You can choose that focus, or you can make an empowering Self-Honoring Choice to switch to the Loving of your Authentic Self and Accept responsibility for the best in you—to own and Accept your Divinity, to own and Accept the Gandhi that resides within you. Spiritual teacher Marianne Williamson so beautifully expressed this in her book *A Return to Love*:

> Our deepest fear is not that we are inadequate. Our deepest fear is that we are powerful beyond measure. It is our light, not our darkness, that most frightens us. We ask ourselves, who am I to be brilliant, gorgeous, talented, and fabulous? Actually, who are you not to be? You are a child of God. Your playing small doesn't serve the world. There's nothing enlightened about shrinking so that other people won't feel insecure around you. We are all meant to shine, as children do. We were born to make manifest the glory of God that is within us. It's not just in some of us; it's in everyone. And as we let our own light shine, we unconsciously give other people permission to do the same. As we are liberated from our own fear, our presence automatically liberates others.

## *The Transformational Power of Awakening*

It's important to remember that as you Awaken, you wake up into the Awareness that you are One with God—and in that moment, you find your true Freedom. Awakening is simply another way of describing the process of remembering that who or what you are is a Divine Loving Being. The more you Awaken, the more you express in a manner we might say is Gandhi-esque.

Have you ever noticed that people who inspire you seem to have an unusual Presence about them—a kind of quality that exudes out and enters you in a positive transforming way?

I (Ron) first witnessed the results of this kind of phenomenon in a man I met many years ago named Sadhu Grewal. He was from India, and he told me that when he was a young man, Gandhi would occasionally visit rural villages to hear people's concerns. A chair was usually set up in the public square, and local residents would line up for miles waiting their turn to speak with him. It often took many hours—sometimes days—before one was actually able to speak with Gandhi.

Sadhu, who was a rather militant sort, decided that he would wait in line and give Gandhi a piece of his mind. He wanted to let this leader know all the things that were wrong in the government and what he should do to make them right. As he waited, his energy of malcontent grew.

Finally, after many hours of waiting, it was Sadhu's turn. He was agitated and impatient to speak as he rushed up to Gandhi. But the moment Sadhu looked into his eyes, he experienced the power of Gandhi's Love flood through him and simply fell to his knees sobbing. All his right/wrong judgmental energy drained out of him instantly, and in its place he was filled with the exquisite Peace of Divine Love. In that moment, he discovered his life's purpose, and he committed to being a disciple of Gandhi, spending the rest of his life traveling as an emissary of Love—which was what he had been doing for more than 40 years when I met him.

The process that Sadhu experienced was the letting go of his right/wrong agenda, which was the cause of his anger, frustration, and rage that led to years of emotional disturbance and suffering. He released his judgments in one glorious moment of surrender and found himself at Home in the Peace of God—where he resided for the remainder of his life. He was Singing his Soul's Song—the song he came to sing.

### *Seeing and Accepting the Majesty of Your Soul*

Make no mistake. The potentiality of qualities, giftedness, and Authentic Self expressions of any other person you experience as inspirational are also Alive inside of you. They are ready to come into Being, into Authentic Self-Expression, as you Awaken. If this were not so, there would be no way for you to recognize those qualities and gifts in someone else.

Quite literally, inspiration means the act of breathing in. As we've mentioned, the word *psyche* means "breath," "principle of life," "Soul." Psychology was originally intended to be the study of the Soul. It was intended to help human beings remember who they are and why they are here: Divine Beings with an Earth School Curriculum designed to assist them in waking up into Soul Awareness. We consider the deep intentions of Spiritual Psychology as restoring the field of psychology to the Spiritual Context and assisting in the greater Awakening of humanity at this time.

If you are reading this, you are likely one of those who is Awakening. We acknowledge you for your Strength of Heart, intention, and commitment. You have, no doubt, been realizing that inspirational moments evoking inner experiences of deeper Meaning, Purpose, or Fulfillment are not to be found externally in physical-world reality.

Yes, it's important to engage and participate in physical-world reality, as it is the stage upon which the game of life is played. Simultaneously, you become more aware of the deeper Spiritual longing, the yearning to answer the Calling of your own Heart, to Awaken into Spiritual Reality, and fulfill your entelechy—in other words, to *Sing Your Soul's Song.*

### *Fulfilling Your Entelechy*

Are you familiar with the word *entelechy*? Simply stated, it's the actualization of potential. Used here, it means "the full realization and expression of your Soul Essence in your human form." The entelechy of an acorn is to become an oak tree. Consider, then, what is your entelechy?

We answer that question in two ways. First, it is your entelechy to realize yourself as a pure emanation of Divine Love. Second, it is your entelechy to stand up in your Authentic Self, sharing your gifts with the world.

What moves your Heart and stirs your Soul? What experiences and expressions do you Love? What brings you Alive? Perhaps it's creative expression through music, poetry, art, dance, or literature. It could be participating in service. For some, it will be speaking with others and bringing forward the Strength of your Heart. For others, it is coaching people in fulfilling their Heartfelt dreams. The short answer is that it's nothing less than *daring to live into your dreams*. The form is not important. What matters is answering the Calling of Spirit in your Heart!

As one USM student reflected on the recent death of a friend, she had this to say about answering the Call: "No one knows how long we'll be here. No one knows what gifts have been lost to all humankind because of someone believing in their limitations instead of their magnificence. That is true tragedy . . . The lesson I am learning is to not wait until I know my death is imminent to share my gifts with the world. I have already waited long enough."

Remember, the only time is *now*!

## THIS CHAPTER'S PRACTICES

The Practices included in this chapter are offered with our Heartfelt encouragement to you to stand forward in the Strength of your Heart and share the Soul Essence of who and what you are: the Presence of Love!

### *Who Inspires You?*

Follow the process in the section of this chapter "Who Inspires You?" Write in your journal your responses regarding a person who inspires you in service to Accepting your Divinity, Awakening more fully into the Awareness of your Essential Loving Nature, and living more fully into your life's purpose.

1.  Who is the person? What do they represent to you?

2.  What is it about them that inspires you? Is it a quality, something about their character, or something they contributed or accomplished?

3.  What is the experience that is evoked inside of you when you think of this person?

4. If you give that experience a voice, what would it say? As a way of owning and accepting the experience and the qualities, make statements out loud beginning with "I am."

5. Can you think of any ways you can take action that would be a living demonstration of your expressing these qualities? What are they?

6. Actually express out loud, or write down, a description of yourself taking these steps in the present. (Note that you are not committing to doing anything beyond this process.)

## 12 Actionable Keys for Living into Your Purpose Here and Now

Review these 12 keys. Then, over a period of the next few weeks, conduct experiments engaging in any or all of them. Write what you do and the experiences you have in your journal.

1. Set your intention to live a life of purpose and meaning, answering and honoring the Calling of your Heart. Write down your intentions for recognizing, aligning with, and living into your purpose. Keep them where you can review them daily or on some kind of regular basis.

(Remember the power of Heartfelt intentions: At their best, intentions become a Heartfelt prayer, a request for Spirit's assistance. You might want to review Chapter 2, "The Power of Clear Intention.")

2. Move into your Heart and reverently ask Spirit, "Given my experience, abilities, gifts, and skills, please show me, in a way I can recognize and understand, how I may best serve." (This can be a beautiful way to complete your day prior to sleep, and a wonderful way to receive inner guidance regarding your purpose.)

3. Surrender your ego's story of victimization, lack, and unworthiness. If you find yourself caught in the ego's old story, take time to Write and Burn it as a way of letting it all go. Remember that your words are a powerful part of how you create your future.

4. Choose to live into your new story of purpose, meaning, and Heart. Do those things you Love to do, *and* do your best to bring Loving to all that you do. Love is the most powerful attractor field. Living in Loving elevates your consciousness and is a powerful vehicle for recalibrating your life to your next levels of experience and expression.

5. Let go of negative self-talk and self-judgment. Change your inner channel from the ego's story of limitation and lack to an inner dialogue with your Authentic Self through Compassionate Self-Forgiveness. Over time, as you practice this skill, you'll gain access to the Presence and gifts of your Authentic Self—and to deeper Awareness of your purpose on both the Goal Line and Soul Line of life.

6. Take time in the Silence. Become receptive and Listen to the whispers of Spirit in your Heart. Actually Listen in the Silence for 5 to 15 minutes (or more). Then journal your Awareness about your unique interests and gifts, as well as those experiences and expressions in which you find Purpose, Meaning, Joy, and Fulfillment. Allow Spirit's guidance to inform your choices.

7. Nurture yourself and your Heartfelt dreams through cultivating positive, supportive, and encouraging self-talk. Engage with people and experiences that inspire you and bring you into fuller Awareness of the goodness and greatness of who you are.

8. Take one small step each day in service to answering the Calling of your Heart. It has been said that the Universe rewards action, not thinking. So create a daily challenge for yourself, and take one step each day in service to living into greater meaning and purpose in your life.

9. Bring forward the Strength of your Heart and be willing to take risks. (As ice hockey great Wayne Gretzky said, "You miss 100 percent of the shots you don't take.")

10. Cultivate a daily Practice of Gratitude and Graciousness: Gratitude to Spirit for the gift of life and all the Blessings you receive; Gratitude for the opportunities to Awaken, share your gifts, and be of service; Gratitude to others for all they contribute; and Gratitude and Graciousness toward your Self, embracing both your humanity and your Divinity. This is a very powerful tool to co-create a life of greater meaning and purpose. Write a minimum of five Gratitude statements in your journal at the end of each day.

11. Reflect on the following questions and write the answers in your journal: What moves your Heart and stirs your Soul? What experiences and expression do you Love? What brings you Alive? (Remember that the form is not important; what matters is answering the Calling of your Heart and Singing Your Soul's Song.)

12. Commit to your Awakening. When you Awaken into the Awareness of your True Identity as a Divine Being having a human experience, then your purpose becomes Self-evident.

Be prepared for surprises! Accepting your humanity opens the doorway to Accepting your Divinity and vice versa, for truly they are one and the same.


### Meditation for Remembering Who You Are

Engage in this simple meditation as often as you like:

*Move into your Heart and remember . . . while you have a body, you are not your body . . . While you have thoughts, you are not your thoughts . . . While you have feelings, you are not your feelings . . . And while you have emotions, you are not your emotions . . . Who are you? . . . You are a Center of pure Loving Awareness.*

*Take in a nice deep breath . . . Relax . . . and let it go . . . And with your next breath, Accept that you are a Divine Being with an Earth*

*School Curriculum designed perfectly to support you in Awakening into the Majesty of the Love that you are and living a life of Meaning, Purpose, and Fulfillment.*

## INTENTION

I am answering the Calling of my already Open Heart,
Singing my Soul's Song, enjoying the Purpose, Meaning,
and Fulfillment I experience, sharing my Light,
Loving, and God-given gifts with those around me.

# CHAPTER 21

# LIVING YOUR LIFE
# AS A PRAYER

*"Prayer is an attitude of the heart."*
— LARRY DOSSEY, M.D.

Recently, during a live class weekend that we were facilitating, one of the participants shared his experience of initiating a practice of "continuously" asking Spirit to shed its Light and Loving upon himself and his wife, as well as all areas of his life. This was his daily prayer for several weeks, and he reported breathtaking results.

He and his wife had been experiencing a deep sadness about their relationship for the past year. Spontaneously, this heaviness lifted for them both, and they were restored to the deep Loving, connection, and intimacy that had characterized their 40 years of marriage. He expressed awe, wonder, and profound Gratitude for the Grace they received. We spoke together about the power of living your life as a Prayer—of cultivating the Practice of Prayer as a vehicle for deep listening and for receiving.

Might you take the next two weeks and "continuously" ask Spirit to shed its Light and Loving upon you, your life, and loved ones for the entire time? Well, why not? Are you ready to receive? At the very least, you'll see what happens.

## Prayer: Communing with the Divine— Coming into Loving Resonance

Some people pray to God as if they were specks of dust, approaching a fire so bright that it might burn them if they approach too close. Others approach God knowing that not only is God their best friend—but also their True Nature. Which approach do you think will enhance the likelihood of your hearing what's being transmitted and communicated to you?

In order to answer this question, we must turn to these foundational Principles of Spiritual Psychology, which will inform our exploration of prayer:

- God is everything in existence, both seen and unseen.

- The nature of God is Love.

- Since we are all part of God, our Essential Nature also is Love—and we have the opportunity of *knowing* our Loving Nature experientially, Here and Now.

Prayer is an opportunity to come into Loving Resonance with the Divine—your Soul Essence made manifest in your Authentic Self—and the Universal Love, the Divine Intelligence that infuses all Creation. It provides entrance into communion with the Divine by its very intention. It is a process that brings you into attunement with the music of your Authentic Self through preparing the place, the sacred space to commune with Father Mother God, Lord God of all Creation. As Henry Miller described it, "In the great peace that came over me, I heard the heart of the world beat. I know what the cure is: it is to give up, to relinquish, to surrender, so that our little hearts may beat in unison with the great heart of the world."

Coming into Loving Resonance results in a depth and fullness, richness and beauty, meaning and purpose in your experience in everyday life. It opens a doorway to communion with the Divine.

Say that word aloud, *resonance*. Even the sound the word makes in your throat connotes what coming into Resonance is all about.

There's a richness of vibrational frequency that resounds, creating an experience of oneness—a Peace and Wholeness within. Coming into Resonance with Your Authentic Self is like coming into Oneness with the Sound of a powerful tone: the music of your Heart, the Song of your Soul that connects you with the Heart of God. The vibrational frequency of the Authentic Self is Unconditional Loving—that is its energetic Essence. Peace . . . Acceptance . . . Aliveness . . . Enthusiasm . . . Compassion . . . Forgiveness . . . Gratitude . . . Joy . . . Happiness . . . Wholeness . . . Holiness . . . Freedom . . . all are harmonics of that High Note and all are in resonance with each other.

We recently attended a memorable evening of music in an architecturally beautiful church in Santa Monica. The program included Mozart's "Ave Verum Corpus" and "Requiem" presented by accomplished professional musicians and vocalists. The completion of the evening was with a Spirit-filled exultation of "The Lord's Prayer." The conductor invited—even challenged—the audience to *feel* the piece and sing along. As I (Mary) listened, the words became my own prayer, resonating deeply within my Heart. My Soul moved me into Loving Resonance with the Divine.

Imagine completing your day with an evening prayer in which you envision yourself being cradled in the arms of Divine Love all night long. That, in and of itself, is a breathtaking prospect. It means releasing your addiction to the familiarity of ego-referenced five-sense reality and opening yourself up to nothing less than the miraculous: to your own personal relationship with the Precious Presence, with the Divine. You'll discover not only that you are Loved, but also that your inherent nature is Loving.

For myself, I find that prayers of Heartfelt Gratitude seem to consistently bring me into connection with the Divine. And sometimes the experience of prayer has no words—rather, it is simply the experience Miller described—sweet surrender knowing that Love is all that is.

### Creating a Light and Loving List

Creating a Light and Loving List is a simple Practice of prayer that can be of great Spiritual support in your Awakening. On this list, you can include the names of any people, animals, or situations that you like. Then, each day, you place all the items on the list into the Light and Love of Spirit for the Highest Good of All Concerned.

Simply put, this is a Practice of asking for Spirit's assistance, guidance, blessings, and inspiration, while releasing your attachment to any particular outcome. This is also a beautiful opportunity to share Gratitude with Spirit for the Gifts and Blessings of Your Life.

On this list, you can include yourself, your family members, your friends, your pets, people who are part of your community, individuals you know who are experiencing particular challenges, situations you're experiencing as difficult or challenging, a particular addiction you'd like to release, and anything else.

If you are intending to make a job or career change, you can include that. If you're preparing to travel and wish to send the Light ahead of you for your trip—include it. If you're intending to move your home or relocate to another city, add it.

If you're experiencing a challenge releasing your judgments against yourself or someone else, you can place a request on your list for Spirit's assistance in releasing your hurt feelings, anger, resentment, and judgments. You can include local, national, or global situations—you get the idea. Some people include a prayer for Peace.

Then simply write your list. And place yourself at the top of the list!

### Placing Yourself and Important Decisions into the Light for the Highest Good

Another powerful Practice is that of placing yourself and your important decisions into the Light of Living Love, asking that you be shown and guided by Spirit in a way that you can recognize and understand what choice is for your Highest Good. Do this whenever you think of the decision, situation, and people involved; it's a tremendous antidote to worry.

This Practice supports releasing ego attachment and surrendering the outcome to Spirit, while trusting that what unfolds is truly for your Highest Good. It's a way of bringing your Heart into Loving Resonance with the Great Heart of the Universe. As our friend Michael Hayes is fond of saying, "Work like it's all up to you; pray like it's all up to God."

I (Mary) began this Practice soon after meeting Ron. My previous relationship had provided excellent learning opportunities for me about the emotionally painful consequences of ego creation. Now I decided it was time for me to conduct a different kind of relationship experiment and began placing my relationship with Ron in the Light. I asked for Spirit's assistance in releasing any attachment to the outcome of our relationship; I asked for only that which was truly for my Highest Good to be brought forward. As evidenced by the path that unfolded, this Practice has served me quite well indeed. I suspect Ron would agree.

We encourage you to engage in this Practice of trusting that Spirit has your best interests (Highest Good) at Heart and directly invite Spirit to participate in the Awakening of your consciousness and in the matters of your daily life. It's another way of aligning ourselves to participate consciously in the co-creative process, recognizing that God is your partner. The possibilities here are endless.

### Speaking Kind Words— A Practice for Living Your Life as a Prayer

The Dalai Lama said, "Be kind whenever possible. It is always possible." I (Mary) find this message to be so potent, so aligned with the True North of my Authentic Self, it's as though an instantaneous attitude adjustment takes place whenever I hear it. I'm brought more into the Awareness of my Essential Loving Nature and the Self-Honoring choices I am capable of making, which are a reflection and expression of my Soul. It's like my Inner Teacher has spoken, and I snap to attention—the small self of my mind and emotions recedes into the wings, and my ever-present, already Loving Heart in all its Goodness, Godness, and full Glory steps center stage.

As you begin living your life inside the Spiritual Context and are less frequently experiencing yourself as an "upset looking for a good because," your healing and transformation provide you with the opportunity to live your life as your best Self. In fact, consider establishing the wholehearted intention to live your life as your best Self—a Beneficial Presence—the Presence of Loving Kindness! That could surely be a game changer.

Imagine that your intention—which is a form of prayer—is to Speak Kind Words. Wean yourself from any expression that is less than kind. Wean yourself from emotional reactivity and out-of-balance expression. What if instead you were to simply slooow down so you can explore the s p a c e between stimulus and response—s p a c e in which you can choose your response and the energy upon which your words ride?

What if Loving becomes the carrier pigeon delivering your message? Would that rock your world?

There are so many opportunities to bring forward the Strength of your Heart through speaking kind words. What if this Way of Being became part of your own code of honor and an expression of Loyalty to Your Soul, something that you choose as a natural way of Living Your Life as a Prayer? "What goes around comes around" is indeed how the Universe works.

Recently, in a live class at the University, one student shared about a co-worker she encountered early in her professional life whom she experienced as the embodiment of Loving Kindness. The co-worker's ways and words had so inspired this student that 15 years later, she continued to share the legacy of Love that her co-worker had shared with her and others.

As someone once said, "The flowers of all the tomorrows are planted in the seeds of today." What beautiful seeds this student is sowing, and what a glorious harvest she is already reaping. May your Loving Kindness and your Kind Words be the seeds you sow and nurture today.

Know that as you bring Blessings to those around you, you are indeed blessed. Consider your Practice of Prayer as one of the most powerful ways you can experience your already open Heart and know yourself as the Presence of Love.

## ⟨ THIS CHAPTER'S PRACTICES ⟩

### *Engage in Daily Prayer*

Write a simple prayer to use upon awakening as you start each day. You may also want to write another prayer for use just prior to going to sleep. It's also fine to just spontaneously express what's present in your Heart, rather than committing to a particular set of words.

If you like this Practice, by all means continue using it beyond this week. From time to time you may want to change or update your prayer.

### *Write, Then Use a Light and Loving List*

Create your very own personal Light and Loving List. We recommend writing a simple prayer at the beginning of your Light List as a beautiful way to begin. Here's an example of a Light List Invocation:

"Just now, Centering my Awareness in my Heart, I give Gratitude for all the Blessings of my life, and I place myself, all people, and items on my Light and Loving List into the Light of Living Love. I ask for Spirit's gracious assistance in all areas of my life, and ask that only that which is for my Highest Good and the Highest Good of all concerned be brought forward."

Don't forget to put yourself at the top of the list! Then, at least once a day, place all the items on your List into the Light. Some people do this Practice in the morning and evening.

### *Place Activities and Decisions into the Light for the Highest Good*

Throughout the day, place yourself, important activities, and decisions into the Light for the Highest Good. It's a great antidote to worry and negative future fantasy. Examples of specific situations you can place in the Light for the Highest Good include:

- Before starting your car, you can surround, protect, and fill yourself, your passengers, and your automobile with the Light, and send Light ahead of you to other drivers on the road, the route, and so on, for the Highest Good.

- Ask for the Presence of the Light during specific meetings; place the agenda items and all those participating into the Light for the Highest Good.

- Ask for time warps in your favor when the amount of time you perceive to be needed in order to accomplish something is less than what is available. You may be presently surprised at how this one works.

- One of Ron's favorites is asking what he calls his "Parking Angels" to lead him to a parking space close to his destination. I (Mary) am amazed at how this works for him.

- Place any decision for which you're requesting Spirit's guidance into the Light, asking to be shown and guided in ways that you can recognize and understand what is for your Highest Good.

## *Speaking Kind Words*

Cultivate the Practice of walking through your life as the Presence of Loving Kindness through Speaking Kind Words. Speak Kind Words with yourself, your partner, children, co-workers, neighbors, boss . . . you get the idea. As Seneca said, "Wherever there is a human being, there is an opportunity for kindness." Write about your experiences in your journal.

### INTENTION

I am communing with the Divine, offering Heartfelt prayers to Spirit, placing myself, my family, my pets, my Awakening, and all people, circumstances, and situations into the Light for the Highest Good of All Concerned.
I am sharing Gratitude for the Blessings of my Life.
I am the Presence of Love, living my life as a Prayer.

# CHAPTER 22

# THE "C" WORD

*"Until one is committed, there is hesitancy, the chance
to draw back, always ineffectiveness. Concerning all acts
of initiative (and creation), there is one elementary truth,
the ignorance of which kills countless ideas and splendid plans:
that the moment one definitely commits oneself, then
Providence moves too. All sorts of things occur to help one
that would never otherwise have occurred. A whole stream
of events issues from the decision, raising in one's favor all manner
of unforeseen incidents and meetings and material assistance,
which no man could have dreamed would have come his way."*
— WILLIAM HUTCHISON MURRAY

The "C" word . . . Hmmm . . . That must mean . . . I know—*chocolate!*

Actually, we sometimes refer to *Commitment* as the "C" word, as many people find themselves reluctant to commit. Yet Commitment is a key to both your Awakening and your Authentic Empowerment in your everyday life. It has powerful reverberations on both the Goal Line and Soul Line.

What, then, is Commitment? As we work with it, Commitment is a state of dedicated engagement. It goes beyond talking the talk; it means walking the walk. It's a process of actualizing your words by taking congruent action. It means a gathering of your energy toward a specified goal or outcome. It also means giving your word in trust.

Honoring a commitment involves taking an action you've agreed to take. And the most powerful aspect of honoring commitments is that *you become One with Your Word.* And in so doing, you experience greater Wholeness; you reside in your Integrity.

## Benefits of Honoring Commitments to Self and Others

Recently we participated in a spiritual retreat in which each segment began with video footage of a cheetah running at full speed. Witnessing the cheetah's power and majesty in slow motion was both mesmerizing and inspiring. As the cheetah ran flat out, 60 miles per hour, it was the embodiment of singleness of purpose and Grace. It was demonstrating 100 percent commitment.

Commitments to oneself are often the most challenging to keep, yet they are the ones with the greatest potential to make a difference in your life. The process of making agreements with yourself and following through with them affirms you in experientially knowing that you can count on you to keep your word with yourself. This builds Self-Trust, Self-Confidence, and Self-Respect. It is a demonstration of Self-Love. It's wonderful to know that you can count on yourself to show up for yourself, especially in challenging times that may require you to go the extra mile inwardly and/or outwardly in either your personal or professional life.

Insofar as honoring agreements with your spouse or partner, when you are on time and do what you say you'll do, it pays huge dividends in the intimacy department. Your partner will feel cared for, cherished, and loved. Keeping your agreements by honoring your commitments is a powerful message that says, "I care. You matter—our relationship is precious to me." It doesn't need to be a grand gesture. One way that I (Mary) receive this message is through a simple act of giving. Ron, after his workout at the club, always remembers to bring home a chai latte for me. My Heart is touched by his kindness, and it reinforces my experience of his Loving and my knowing that I can count on him—that he is here for me.

In your work life, honoring commitments is a path to being highly regarded and respected. It often leads to greater responsibility and authority as well as compensation increases and performance bonuses. You'll be recognized and appreciated by your co-workers as a team player, and your approach to your work will be known as producing successful results. We count on our staff who consistently do what they say they will do, and do it with Loving Excellence.

In your Spiritual life, commitment is essential because Spiritual Awakening is generally a process, not a single event!

One of our friends, a highly successful executive coach, shared that his high-end coaching practice really took off when he began consistently honoring his 90-minute daily commitment to himself, which consisted of Spiritual Practice and vigorous physical activity. He became very disciplined in his commitment; and through demonstrating leadership in his own life, the by-product was that he naturally showed up as a leader for others.

One commitment that I (Mary) have made with myself is to write when Spirit wakes me up in the middle of the night. I know that when I do so it is magical, as it provides me time in the Silence to receive Spirit's inspiration—to connect with my muse. More globally, I love the inner sense of well-being I experience from honoring my commitments to myself and others. There's an inner Peace that follows. I also appreciate how renegotiating agreements with others is such a demonstration of respect and caring for myself and for them.

### The Price of Not Keeping Commitments

The price tags for not honoring commitments include the erosion of trust with both yourself and others; physical and emotional stress that drains your energy through the incomplete cycles of actions; and loss of Self-Respect, Self-Confidence, and Self-Trust. In some cases, the consequences are financial, such as late fees, additional interest, and the loss of credit or bonuses. Perhaps the biggest cost to not keeping your commitments is the erosion of your sense of Self-Worth.

So what should you do when you don't keep your word to yourself or someone else? The first key is this: If you recognize in advance that you're not going to be able to keep your word, proactively initiate communication with the other parties involved and renegotiate the timeline. This is not only considerate; it builds trust. Similarly, if you become aware you're going to be late to a commitment, call the person involved to advise them that you're going to be late.

This may bring to mind the specifics of certain broken agreements with yourself or others. "What about all those broken agreements that I have with myself? All the mornings I've rolled over to go back to sleep rather than get up and work out? What about the money I borrowed from my dad that I haven't paid back? What about the commitment I made to my daily spiritual practice that I haven't honored? What about all the times I've told my spouse I'll be home by 6 P.M. for dinner, but didn't show up until 7 P.M. or later?" Whatever the details, we applaud you for your Self-Honesty in acknowledging them.

When it comes to broken commitments or agreements with others, first decide whether you're ready to honor the agreement. If you are, clarify a plan to which you're ready to commit, and then either write or call the person to let them know of your new commitment. Be sure to follow through in a timely way. In the case of owing money, for example, you could either send full repayment or offer installments on the original debt.

The most important thing is to wipe the slate clean through acknowledging the broken agreement. If you have judgments about yourself, the situation, or the others involved, let the judgments go. Holding them against yourself and making yourself wrong will only make it harder to honor your word and keep your commitments going forward.

Begin again here and now. Consider making a commitment to honoring your word and consciously tracking your agreements with yourself and others so that they are in your awareness. You can make it your priority to keep your agreements as part of the discipline of Becoming One with Your Word; know that the dividends this investment can pay will be endless.

*Important key:* You are much better off not committing to something you are not sure you can honor rather than committing and then not honoring your agreement.

## Your Most Important Commitment— Committing to Your Awakening

Your most sacred commitment might be the fulfillment of the Spiritual Contract you made prior to entering the Earth School. What did you come here to learn? What is your Soul's Purpose in being here? What talents or abilities do you have that are part of the gift you've come to give—and to what degree are you giving of them? What commitments does being Loyal to Your Soul usher into action?

Consider this: What if your primary spiritual agenda or purpose in this lifetime *is your own Awakening?* In other words, living your life Awake to the Love that is your Essential Nature—that is, who and what you are? Would that shift your perspective and priorities? What if you made a commitment to live your life as the Presence of Love?

I (Mary) wear a little beaded bracelet with a Love charm as a way of reminding myself to live as the Presence of Love. Being with Ron reminds me. Our sweet little kitty, Darling Isabella, and her purrrrrring reminds me moment to moment. Spending time in the stillness of my rose garden reminds me. And on it goes. In fact, I realize my life has been set up as one giant "Note to Self": You are the Presence of Love; now be it.

A few years ago, while we were visiting with a friend in New Mexico, a gentleman we had known years before was invited to join us for an afternoon of tea. Although he didn't stay too long, what was notable in our conversation was the sweetness of Loving, the complete devotion, reverence, and respect that were present as he spoke of a friend. His life was about caring for this woman who was now experiencing Alzheimer's. For some years, he had been her caregiver 24/7, although she no longer knew who he was. He, however, knew who she was to him, and perhaps more profoundly, he was choosing to faithfully answer and honor his Soul's call to Love. His commitment to seeing her through was characterized by his devotion to serving her in Unconditional Loving. In that moment we were privileged to be witnessing a truly beautiful and poignant Love Story.

### Answering Your Soul's Calling

What is your Soul's Calling? Are you committed to answering the call to Awake to Love? Reading this book and participating in the Practices is surely a demonstration of your commitment to Awakening into the reality of your Authentic Self—your inherently Loving Nature—and of learning and applying skills that support you in your Authentic Empowerment and Living the Loving in your everyday life. We acknowledge you and the Commitment to your Self you are already demonstrating.

Is there another commitment to yourself, perhaps one related to your Awakening or to your physical-world reality, that you'd like to consider at this time? Perhaps there's a Heartfelt goal you'd like to commit to moving into manifestation. Or perhaps there's a commitment to treating yourself differently. Or perhaps you are called to make a deeper commitment to your Awakening.

This chapter's Practice includes simple steps you can use to support you in identifying and following through with a new commitment that you would like to make. Remember, commitment and keeping agreements are not about perfection; they're about Awareness, Loving excellence, and the automatic benefits of Becoming One with Your Word. To paraphrase Goethe: "Whatever you can do, or dream you can, begin it. Boldness has genius, power, and magic in it. Begin it now."

These simple and empowering steps can be used to support yourself in (1) identifying an area of your life where you'd like to move forward, such as with your Awakening or another matter, (2) clarifying your specific commitments, and (3) tracking and honoring your commitments.

To enhance the likelihood of your success, remember this very important key: *Be very specific with your commitments.*

For example, rather than committing to a general idea like "getting more exercise," commit to a specific training program or to exercising once a week for a minimum of 30 minutes. Rather than committing to "being more Loving with yourself," commit to having an inner conversation with yourself of a prizing and supportive nature at least twice a week. If you intend to pray or meditate more, you can commit to praying or meditating for a specific time period once a day for a week. You get the idea.

### Clarifying Your Intention and Commitment

Step 1: Identify an area of your life that is important to you and in which you'd like to move forward. State this as an intention.

Step 2: Identify one specific action step (a baby step) you can take, if you choose, which you believe would move you closer to having or experiencing what you say you would like to have or experience.

Step 3: In the inner eye of your imagination, envision yourself enthusiastically taking the action step.

Step 4: From a place of inner freedom, ask yourself, "Am I willing to commit to taking this specific action step on a timeline of my own choosing?"

Step 5a: If you're not ready to make a commitment at this time, that's just fine. Perhaps there's another commitment that is more doable for you now. Acknowledge and appreciate yourself for your willingness to explore the area of commitment. Restart the steps another day.

Step 5b: If you're ready to make a commitment, write it down. Acknowledge and appreciate yourself for your willingness to move forward.

Step 6: Each day throughout this week, hold the intention to be One with Your Word. Be intentional about the agreements/commitments you make and keep them.

Step 7: Journal your experience, tracking the commitments or agreements you make and keep. Acknowledge and appreciate yourself for those you keep. Observe those you don't keep; it's important to explore what it is that you are making more important than Becoming One with Your Word.

## INTENTION

I am answering my Soul's call to Awaken Unto Love,
cultivating the Practice of becoming One with My Word,
consciously making and honoring my agreements with myself
and others. I am honoring my commitment
to live my life as the Presence of Love.

CHAPTER 23

# UNWORTHINESS: A CASE OF MISTAKEN IDENTITY

*"What is your trouble? Mistaken identity."*

— WEI WU WEI

Let's be clear! You are a Divine Being using a human experience for the purpose of Awakening. This being the case, we have an important question for you: Have you come to the place where you are willing to let go of your misidentification of yourself as unworthy and unlovable in service to waking up more fully in the Awareness of the *Loving Essence* that you truly are?

Unworthiness is simply a case of mistaken identity. It's a case of attempted identity theft by your ego. You may be asking, "How does this happen, and what can I do about it?" Here goes!

### The Ego's Story of Misidentification

The ego creates a story in order to have a sense of identity inside the space-time continuum of physical-world reality. Due to the dualistic nature of the mind and emotions, it has a self-created story of suffering infused with limitation, lack, unhappiness, and a deep misidentification with unworthiness. This mythology is fabricated—perhaps we could even say hallucinated—by the ego based on its dualistic and judgmental approach to life. This approach is restrictive and limited, built upon the ego's matrix of beliefs and the distortions that exist within your perceptual filter in combination with the ego's propensity to judge. This is further amplified through the ego's attachment to maintaining the illusions of the ego patterns of comfort, security, and control. In other words, your ego has been installed with a faulty navigation system.

It's important to remember that your ego is a *tool* and not who you are. It's always working with the picture you hold in mind of your goals and what you've been conditioned to believe. What you define as success in a particular area is the blueprint that you provide for your ego to fulfill. Although your ego will do its best to achieve your ideal image, its primary concern is self-importance and its most limiting characteristic is inflexibility. It's your ego that tends to keep you caught in the familiarity of your comfort zone.

Let's take a second look at what we refer to as the Anatomy of Beliefs, as it provides a window into understanding how this faulty navigating system operates.

- Emotional reactions are physiological responses to thoughts and perceptions.

- Thoughts and perceptions are subjective and a function of beliefs.

- Beliefs are composed of interpretations of early experience learned in accordance with your Spiritual Curriculum.

- What you believe determines your experience, including your emotions.

It follows that if you think and believe you're unworthy, you'll *feel* unworthy, and you'll behave in ways that *express unworthiness*. Your Universe will reflect your unworthiness to you, thus reinforcing your sense of yourself as unworthy. It's a never-ending cycle where you always return to your starting point of perceived unworthiness, continuing until the day you choose to change it. Doing so takes Awareness, clarity of intention, and courageous action to liberate your self from the misidentification of being unworthy.

## *Releasing the Shroud of Perceived Unworthiness*

You may be asking, "How do I let go of this shabby shroud painted with the unattractive colors of self-doubt, self-judgment, self-rejection, and self-loathing? I am shackled to the misidentification of myself as unworthy, bound to my misidentification with the small, restricted self of my ego. How do I release the deep sense of shame and guilt that binds me to this worn-out cloak of unworthiness that no longer fits?"

Many years ago during a five-day seminar, we had the privilege of witnessing a man suddenly being filled with the Light of Spirit. He actually fell to the floor; some minutes later, as he slowly got to his feet, his face was glowing—illuminated by Light. He put out his hand in gesture to those of us present and said, "We are not meant to live as beggars on this planet." People around us began to sob, as he spoke from the place of his Soul Essence.

This man suddenly and fully released the shroud of perceived unworthiness—he simply let it go. All present were blessed, and his enlightenment set off a chain of events in which Spirit moved through the group. The memory of this experience is forever etched in our Hearts, as it is a profound reference point for remembering who we truly are—inherently worthy, Divine.

The seminar completed the next day, and it was another two years before we saw the man again. We greeted him warmly, recalling the Blessing of his Illumination, and communicated that we had missed him. He shared with us that it had taken all this time for him to integrate the experience he had—to fully Accept and live into the Blessing.

## Shifting Gears: Ego-Referenced Thinking and Authentic Self–Referenced Thinking

Once you learn to discern the difference between ego-referenced and Authentic Self–Referenced Thinking within your own consciousness, you can more easily recognize when you are limiting yourself by falling into the mythology of mistaken identification with unworthiness. Then you can actively take dominion within your mind, moving from the consciousness of the false self to the consciousness of the True Self.

Learning this skill paves the way for shortening the time spent in the self-torture of mental anguish and emotional suffering. The natural result is that you are free to live life more fully, experiencing your Self as a Soul having a human experience. You realize that you are Divine, you are Unconditional Love, and your body is a Temple for your Soul. Taking dominion within your own consciousness by choosing what thoughts you entertain and what identification you hold is part of spiritual ecology, and it is a deeply Self-Honoring choice.

*Clues for recognizing ego-referenced thinking:* right/wrong thinking; blaming others; hearing yourself telling your story as a victim story; emotional upset, reactivity, and negativity; judgment of self, others, or situations; and any self-talk that holds you into the misidentification of yourself as unworthy

*Clues for recognizing Authentic Self–Referenced Thinking:* Exercising the Mother of All Choices through Accepting personal responsibility for your internal environment (your thoughts and feelings); thoughts of an Accepting nature; neutrality; creative responses to others and to situations; remembering who you are, a Divine Being having a human experience and choosing those thoughts, attitudes, and actions that are in harmony with your Inherent Worthiness

## *Taking Dominion within Your Consciousness*

You have been given the capacity to take dominion within your own consciousness and to choose the nature and direction of your own thinking. This is an opportunity for impeccability—meaning right use of your energy. Energy follows thought. What you focus on, you tend to create.

Those negative emotions that stem from beliefs and judgments are possible only in ego-referenced thinking. Our guidance to you here is simple and direct: Don't spend time hanging out in the negativity of ego-referenced thinking about yourself, anyone, or anything. It will not serve you. Authentic Self–Referenced Thinking is a lot more fun; you're promoting experiences of Joy, Peace, Love, Aliveness, Creativity, and Fulfillment.

One of this chapter's Practices provides an opportunity to practice what we refer to as Meta-Thinking, meaning to become Aware of the level of thinking you are engaging in at any given time. This Practice can assist you in developing greater Awareness regarding the nature and direction of your thinking, and the influence of your thinking on your clarity, decisions, and actions. This strengthens your ability to recognize and shift from ego-referenced thinking to Authentic Self–Referenced Thinking.

We encourage you to have fun with this! As Wei Wu Wei put it, "Play your part in the comedy, but don't identify yourself with your role." You're making it all up anyway, so you may as well star in a comedy rather than a tragedy.

## *Shifting Gears: Giving Gratitude and Receiving Grace*

One of my (Mary's) favorite holidays is New Year's Day, as I often find myself seated cozily in front of the fireplace in our family room, enjoying a crackling fire and writing an abundance of Love and Gratitude notes. Even as a young child, my mother had me writing—er, painstakingly composing—my own little hand-printed thank-you notes for gifts received from my grandmothers, and I still find great Joy in writing thank-yous. I notice my consciousness elevates as I move into Loving Resonance with the person I am thanking. I write from my Heart to their Heart.

A delightful quote that I remember from my childhood is from *Winnie-the-Pooh* by A. A. Milne: "Piglet noticed that even though he had a Very Small Heart, it could hold a rather large amount of Gratitude." When I express Gratitude, my "Very Small Heart" becomes quite expanded.

Through this immersion in Giving Gratitude, the Sweetness of the Authentic Self becomes present, and I find myself overflowing with Loving Kindness and Thanksgiving: a state of Grace. I feel renewed and replenished, ready to begin another year of Loving. In the consciousness of Gratitude, there is Abundance, Plenty, the experience of Inner Wealth. There is no thought or feeling of lack or unworthiness.

The wonderful Practice of Receiving is a beautiful way to prepare your Self as an instrument of Giving. The inner wealth of your Authentic Self is here, available to you in unending supply. Forgiveness is the key giving you access to the Sanctuary of your Soul—and to the Peace . . . Love . . . Joy . . . Compassion . . . Acceptance . . . Aliveness . . . Inspiration . . . Wisdom . . . Gratitude . . . Healing Grace . . . Happiness . . . and more that is available for you to receive and share as Blessings of your Awakening.

We encourage you in bringing forward the Strength of Your Heart as you continue releasing anything that is blocking you from the full Awareness of the Love and Light that you are. And if your ego attempts to pick your pocket, to steal your identity and leave behind some facsimile of the false self, know that in truth your Soul is eternal, and no one can ever take that from you. The illusions of the false self are but a mirage—at best, fool's gold.

## THIS CHAPTER'S PRACTICES

### *Meta-Thinking: Becoming Aware of Your Thoughts*

In this Practice, we're going on an excursion inward into a relatively unexplored territory: the domain of your consciousness. Your task will be to observe your thought process and discern as much as possible whether at any given moment, you are engaged in ego-referenced thinking or Authentic Self–Referenced Thinking.

Whenever you notice you're momentarily caught in the negativity, limitation, and lack of ego-referenced thinking, take dominion. Consciously forgive yourself for forgetting who you are, a Divine Loving Being. Then, speaking from your Heart, engage in statements that are an expression of Authentic Self–Referenced Thinking.

Write about your experiences in your journal and about what you are learning from your experience.

### *Expressing Gratitude*

Express Gratitude to your Self, others, and to God. Keep a Gratitude Journal; every day, write a minimum of five statements of appreciation, as a way of cultivating your experience of the Consciousness of Worthiness and Wealth.

### *Gratitude Meditation*

All humanity continuously partakes in a particular Spiritual Grace Flow: We receive life through our breath, and as we draw air into our lungs, we are breathing by Spirit's Grace. You can even go so far as to say that Spirit is breathing you.

In this meditation, we invite you to follow the rising and the falling of your breath while silently chanting the word *Love*. Simply close your eyelids, silently repeating the word *Love* on the in-breath, then repeating the word *Love* on the out-breath . . .

You'll notice the *big Love* of the Universe floods you with Loving as your "Very Small Heart" beats in Grateful resonance. You are nothing less than the Light and Breath of God in human form.

## INTENTION

I am Awakening into the True Gold
of my Authentic Self—Living in the conscious
Awareness of the Love and Worthiness that I am.
I am an instrument of the Divine, Giving Gratitude
and Receiving Grace as the Great Heart of the
Universe floods me with Loving.

# CHAPTER 24

# HITTING A SPIRITUAL HOME RUN

*"For when the One Great Scorer comes to mark against your name,*
*He writes—not that you won or lost—*
*But how you played the game."*

— GRANTLAND RICE

This morning, before I (Mary) began writing this chapter, I was reading some letters from students who are utilizing the Principles and Practices of Spiritual Psychology in their everyday lives. It is through receiving your messages and learning how you are experiencing the process that Ron and I learn how we can respond, continuing to serve you in ways that truly support you in your Awakening.

As I read, once again I realized the importance of this Spiritual Psychology Principle: "The subjective nature of personal internal reality determines perception." Your frame of reference determines how you approach, perceive, understand, and, most important, *choose to respond* to yourself, others, and your experiences. This Principle tells you, in one simple sentence, a truth that, when understood and utilized, gives you *huge* leverage in transforming your consciousness and transforming your life. In plain English, it's a realization that can change everything.

## The Importance of Your
## Internal Frame of Reference

Let's review this dynamic. If your internal frame of reference is built upon a misidentification of yourself as a victim, you will perceive yourself as a victim and at the mercy of circumstances that are beyond your control. You will find yourself judging, blaming, faultfinding, and wrong making. And in so doing, you will either feel righteous, arrogant, and superior, or you will collapse into the false belief of your unworthiness. Your outer experiences will be fraught with disharmony, conflict, hurt feelings, disappointment, anger, missed opportunities, and unhappiness. As you can see, this frame of reference assigns you to a litany of life experiences characterized by self-victimization and chronic "I'm upset because . . ."

Suppose, on the other hand, your internal frame of reference is one of Seeing Through Soul-Centered Eyes and a Learning Orientation to Life in which your intention is Awakening. You will perceive yourself as Empowered, rather than at the effect of outside circumstances beyond your control. You will find yourself Accepting and Cooperating with what is going on in your life. Through your commitment to embracing and living into the Spiritual Context, you'll be aware that the primary purpose of your life is learning and letting go of anything that appears to block you from the Awareness of the Love that you are. In this context, you are free to soar, participating in a life filled with giving and receiving Love.

Awakening happens moment by moment, choice by choice. Reading this book is nothing less than a Spiritual Psychology spring training camp designed with Love to strengthen and support you in Seeing yourself, your Earth School Curriculum, and your life's journey through Soul-Centered eyes.

## *A Spiritual Home Run: Opportunity within Challenge*

As Martin Luther King, Jr., put it, "The ultimate measure of a man is not where he stands in moments of comfort and convenience, but where he stands at times of challenge and controversy." Challenging times are indeed Spirit's way of providing us with opportunities to step up to the plate and hit a Spiritual Home Run.

Within the Spiritual Context, people and situations you experience as difficult are recognized for what they are: your Soul providing you with opportunities to remember that you are a Divine Being having a human experience and so is everyone else! These experiences are opportunities for choosing Compassion for yourself and for Seeing through the Eyes of Love, opportunities for listening deeply to Spirit's whisperings in your Heart, opportunities for answering the Call to Love.

To understand what a Spiritual Home Run looks like, we must start by recognizing a curveball for what it is: testing time in the Game of Life. Of course, there are those all-too-human moments of striking out in reactivity, and getting benched for arguing with players on the other team, not to mention cursing the umpire.

What all these experiences have in common is that they are feedback in the game of life. They're letting you know your ego is leading you, hypnotizing you, into misidentification of yourself as a victim. When this happens, it's your opportunity to bring in your best batter and recognize the Spiritual opportunity present. Then, when that next "I'm upset because . . ." curveball comes across the plate, seize the opportunity for using Compassionate Self-Forgiveness to knock the ball out of the park!

Compassionate Self-Forgiveness is not for sissies. It takes great courage to acknowledge your upsets, surrender into the Loving, and Forgive yourself for your judgments, misinterpretations of reality, and misidentifications. In the end, what you'll find is that as you round third base, you'll receive a standing ovation from the crowd of angels cheering you on your way Home.

## A Wild Pitch: Mary's Story of a Challenge and Living Inside the Spiritual Context

On November 10, 2009, not even knowing I (Mary) was up to bat, I received an unexpected curveball. I awakened one morning with Ron telling me that he'd experienced pain running down his left arm during the night; however, rather than wake me up, he had observed it and eventually fallen back to sleep.

Well, I immediately suggested that Ron call his good friend and doctor. Ron did not move, so a moment later (though it seemed like a very long time to me), I sprang out of bed, went very quickly downstairs, and called our doctor friend.

Through Grace, our friend answered his phone straight away and, hearing my concern, asked to speak with Ron immediately. He ordered Ron to get dressed, to skip having a shower and breakfast and just go directly to the emergency room. He called ahead to alert the hospital of Ron's imminent arrival and advise them that Ron had very likely had a heart attack.

Ron and I were both in good spirits driving to the hospital. He was experiencing no symptoms, and I was present enough to the situation to be in prayer, asking for Spirit's assistance for Ron's Highest Good. Upon our arrival, the ER attendants swept Ron away to a triage station to take his vitals. The moment the cardiologist arrived, Ron began to experience the very same symptoms he had during the night, and the doctor administered some nitroglycerin tablets.

Shortly, I was alone in the room with Ron, and I observed him turning quite gray in color. Needless to say, this was very alarming to me. My stomach in turmoil and my heart in my throat, I quickly went into the hallway, found my way to the nurses' station, and reported my concern, asking for the doctor to come immediately.

At that moment my cell phone rang. It was our doctor friend, telling me he was parking his car and wanting to know our location in the hospital. It seemed that both he and the cardiologist appeared simultaneously in Ron's room. They were in agreement that Ron must have an angiogram immediately to determine whether any of his arteries were blocked and, if so, to what degree.

While Ron was wheeled up to the "cath lab," I was escorted to a small private waiting room adjacent to it. As I sat alone, I made several phone calls, asking that Ron be placed on various Light Lists. I spoke with our staff and shared with them what was happening, asking for their Light and Love.

Suddenly, everything began happening quickly. The cardiologist and our doctor friend reappeared and sat down across from me. The cardiologist stated that three of Ron's arteries were significantly blocked and that he needed triple bypass surgery immediately. Now everything was unfolding in slow motion.

My cell phone rang, and in that moment the synchronicity was staggering; it was my internist returning my earlier call. He asked the name of the surgeon who would do the procedure and told me he would check him out. After just a few moments, he rang back to let me know that the surgeon was head of a team considered to be number one in the state of California for this type of bypass surgery. I signed the papers.

By this time, a dear friend had arrived to be with me, and we were given a moment with Ron while they prepped him for the surgery. I called our healer and held the phone to Ron's ear that he might aid in preparing Ron for surgery. Then we began our vigil of Light, Prayer, chanting, and holding a vision of the best possible outcome for Ron's Highest Good, knowing that my deepest prayer was that he choose to continue his life here in the Earth School. Another beloved friend arrived to sit with me, holding in the Loving.

After several hours, the surgeon came out to tell me that the surgery was complete and Ron had done very well. After more time, Ron was wheeled out of the operating room. I was able to see him with my own eyes and feel him with my Heart and hands. I felt relieved that the surgery was complete, and also aware that Ron was in a vulnerable state.

The head nurse of cardiac care came to meet me and told me that I would be welcome to visit Ron in his room in 45 minutes to meet the nurse who would be caring for him through the night. I did wait, and when I met Ron's nurse, I looked deeply into her eyes and knew that she was an amazing Being and that Ron was in *very* good hands physically. I also knew he was in the best of hands spiritually.

I went home in Awareness that Ron could choose to stay or he could choose to go. I lit a candle in our bedroom and called in the Light. I set my alarm early so that I could speak with the night nurse to hear about Ron's process during the night before she went off duty. Then I fell asleep sending Ron Blessings of Loving and Light for his Highest Good. I asked that Ron; those attending Ron, both seen and unseen; and myself be enfolded and held in Spirit's Loving and Light.

When I awakened just before the alarm, I was grateful that there had been no call from the hospital. Thus began a week of long days in the hospital followed by a weekend in class with our second-year students.

Ron's coming home was a process that unfolded like a comedy of errors. It included blowing out all the electricity in our bedroom and ended with me lying down on our bed and laughing, and Ron begging me not to make him laugh as his body hurt when he laughed due to the stitches and staples in his chest. I was happy to see him trying to not laugh, as it was a sure sign that he was doing so much better and hadn't lost his keen sense of humor.

I was kept very present and focused through Loving and supporting Ron and his Healing in combination with teaching three weekends a month without Ron by my side; attending to the operations of the University; and overseeing continued renovations on our home, as our contractor finished putting on a new roof and installing solar panels. Thanksgiving Day came, and what a joyous celebration of Gratitude for Ron's health we enjoyed with friends of the Heart. After a sumptuous, yet heart-healthy dinner, Ron took his first real walk in the neighborhood. Although it was short, all of us were invigorated and encouraged about Ron's full recovery.

Throughout this time, both Ron and I received such an infusion of Light, Loving, and support. Fortunately due to many years of spiritual study and practice through which I'd had the opportunity to strengthen my spiritual muscles, I did not find myself in "I'm upset because . . . ," nor did I observe Ron ever expressing upset or judgment about his heart event, hospitalization, or the months of his extended recovery. In fact, the day after the operation, I asked Ron what he wanted me to tell everyone. He simply said, "Tell them it's a good thing."

For myself, I was very aware of residing in the Strength of my Heart. I somehow moved into Spiritual Warrior consciousness, which brought clarity regarding my intention, impeccability about how I used my energy, and ruthlessness in my focus of residing in my Loving while being of service to Ron and the others around me. And Ron, throughout his hospitalization and extended recovery, demonstrated the consciousness of Acceptance, somehow innately knowing that this experience, too, was for him.

Years before this event when I was learning lots about how to maintain my equanimity in the face of my upset being triggered, my Spiritual Teacher had said to me with great kindness, "When you're at your worst, I'm at my best." As he spoke those words to me, they went so deeply into my Heart—etched there for eternity as a knowing of the Communion and Oneness that is present and knowable through attuning to Divine Love.

I consider this experience, which went on for several months, a reference point for living inside the Spiritual Context and actively using the Principles and Practices of Spiritual Psychology. Throughout this time, though I didn't know whether Ron would fully recover or whether we would be able to resume our work together, I was vigilant within my own consciousness and did not allow myself the luxury of a negative thought. I remained in the Divine Unknowing, bringing forward the Strength of my Heart, and I held myself accountable to my Self and Ron, and our students, faculty, and staff. Most important, my intention was to be Loyal to my Soul. My everyday life became a stand for Love.

Later, through a trusted Spiritual Advisor, we became aware that Ron had been scheduled to complete his life here and exit the Earth School and had been granted "an extension." Surely, this was a sign of the Goodness and Graciousness of the Divine at work. I consider this a Spiritual Home Run of an entirely different order.

## *Postscript to the Story*

Now here's what we consider the most important part of this story. You'll notice that the way in which I told this story was filled with what might be called "assumptions" and "interpretations" about the meaning of various events and the sense I made of them. In fact, as you were reading it, you may have found yourself thinking, *How does she really know that for sure?* or *This sure doesn't sound like a happy story to me.*

But you know what? There's no way I can "prove" to you that my interpretation is any more or less accurate than yours. Anyway, does it really matter? The fact is that my way of Seeing it is in harmony with the Principles and Practices of Spiritual Psychology; and further, my story is comprised of Loving people committed to Seeing the opportunities and Blessings in all aspects of life.

As our Spiritual Teacher was fond of saying, "It's foolish not to win in your own fantasies." And, as we say in Spiritual Psychology, "How you relate to the issue *is* the issue." More and more medical research these days is correlating positive attitude with positive outcome.

---

### THIS CHAPTER'S PRACTICE

---

## *Your Spiritual Home Run*

Imagine you're up to bat. Identify a challenging pitch that is coming toward you. How can you hit a Spiritual Home Run?

Is there a situation that is providing you an opportunity of this nature? If you showed up as your Best Self and utilized the Principles and Practices you've been learning through reading this book and participating in the Practices, what would that look like? Write about this in detail in your journal.

## INTENTION

I am growing in Self-Compassion, Seeing myself
and my life experiences through Soul-Centered eyes,
knowing it's all *for* me—how I relate to the issue is the issue
and the opportunity. I am Forgiving myself as I am
Remembering who I am—a Soul using a human
experience for purposes of Awakening.

# CHAPTER 25

# SPIRITUAL CRAMPONS: GRIT AND GRATITUDE

*"It is not the critic who counts; not the man who points out how the strong man stumbles, or where the doer of deeds could have done better. The credit belongs to the man who is actually in the arena, whose face is marred by dust and sweat and blood; who strives valiantly; who errs, who comes short again and again, because there is no effort without error and shortcoming; but who does actually strive to do the deeds; who knows great enthusiasms, the great devotions; who spends himself in a worthy cause; who at the best knows in the end the triumph of high achievement, and who at the worst, if he fails, at least fails while daring greatly."*

— THEODORE ROOSEVELT

Awakening is not for the faint of heart! The process can be glorious, sprinkled with magical moments—no, actually, it's more like transcendental experiences of the Soul and way better than the sugar high of your favorite toppings on frozen yogurt. And it can be arduous, rigorous, requiring tenacity, clarity of intention, and purpose—and Spiritual Crampons.

"Oh, my God!" you might be asking, "Did you say 'crampons'? Aren't those for mountain climbing—I'm not sure I'm up for that . . ."

Yes, indeed! Spiritual Crampons will support you in gaining traction and altitude above the slippery slope of the ego's carefully constructed and concealed glacial crevasses of security, comfort, and control, which are designed to keep you in the fear and familiarity of your limiting beliefs and the negative self-talk to be endured in your uncomfortable comfort zone.

"Well, Ron and Mary, what else have you got for me that's going to prepare me for this seemingly daunting, albeit epic, ascent: climbing the Mountain of Light, transforming issues, surrendering my illusions, and Awakening into the Majesty of my Soul—and Singing my Soul Song?"

Well, Beloved One, it will be so helpful to consider that your Soul is eternal, and that your Soul exists both Here and Now in the Precious Presence, and also outside the confines of the illusions of space and time. Consider for a moment that your Soul knows you and is already Awake at the top of the mountain, joyfully sounding its Call of Love, its Hymn to Peace, its Prayer of Gratitude. And, further, you are being Spiritually supported, guided, Loved, and protected as you climb.

Do you remember the yearning? Yes, the Holy longing that started all this? The time when you got down on your knees and prayed? Spirit is answering your prayer to know who you truly are—to know the Divine. Now is not the time to lose Heart, close your Spiritual eyes, and beat a hasty retreat back to the comfort of your cave and your fantasies. As Rumi said, "Let yourself be silently drawn by the stronger pull of what you really love."

"Well, Ron and Mary, I'm thinking that's all well and good, but where do I get Spiritual Crampons? I have a heavy load and I don't even have any mountain guides to help carry my stuff as I make the ascent. Besides, I'm afraid of heights; I get sweaty palms the minute I put my feet on the second rung of a ladder. And what about an ice axe? Am I going to need one of those? I'm not very good with tools."

Ah, Beloved One! Do not be afraid. You don't need to find mountain guides, as you already have 100,000 angels by your side. They are willing to take the burdens of your unresolved issues, attachments, expectations, hurt, grief, and the suffering of your misidentification with your unworthiness as quickly as you are ready to let them go. As for an ice axe, you have heat from the hearth of your Heart radiating Light and warmth in all directions to let you know that you are always at Home. Beloved, your Compassionate Heart is so ready and willing to forgive your judgments so you can fly free, soaring on the Wings of Love.

What you do need is to summon the Grit within you: your indomitable Spirit, your clear intention, tenacity, Strength of Heart, willingness to persevere and endure, resilience, courage, and determination. Climbing the Mountain of Light is a character-building experience. Gird your loins with Grit and Gratitude, and let's go on. The climb is not about the ego gratification that comes from achieving something impressive to add to your résumé; it's about nothing less than the Radiant Joy of Awakening into the Transcendent.

"All right, all right. My mind chatter is busy with 100,000 questions, never mind the 100,000 angels by my side . . . Where on earth am I going to find Spiritual Crampons? I don't even know what crampons look like. Do I need hiking boots? I apologize . . . I don't mean to whine. You were saying . . . ?"

Shhhh, Beloved. No worries. All that is necessary for your triumphant ascent is being provided. For now . . . take a deep breath . . . let it go . . .

Now gently close your eyelids . . . Relax in the Peace that is already present . . . Rest in the Love that gently enfolds and cradles you . . . And breathe in the Loving . . . Ahhhh . . . Receive the Love in all levels of your consciousness . . . in every cell in your body . . .

Father Mother God . . . Lord God of all Creation. We ask just now that we be filled, surrounded, and protected with your Divine Light of Living Love, knowing that your Love is our Love and that our small Hearts beat in resonance with your Heart—the Great Heart of the Universe.

We come before you in ordinariness . . . and in Gratitude for the gift of life, for the opportunities to Awaken—surrendering the concerns of our egos to experientially know our True Nature as Peace . . . Joy . . . and Loving . . .

We give Gratitude for your Presence—for You are truly the Wind beneath our Wings, lifting our Hearts, inspiring our Souls.

We are grateful for the Strength of Heart . . . for the opportunity to ascend the Mountain of Light, to enter the Golden Temple of the Soul, to hear the sounds of the flute . . . poetic and penetrating . . . carrying us higher into the sacred knowing of God/Love.

Like Meister Eckhart, the prayer we say is "thank you." Amen.

Now, in the Silence of your own Heart, relax into Child Pose, kneeling . . . Yes, bowing . . . Yes, offering your own Prayer of Gratitude. Knowing, as William Blake knew, "Gratitude is Heaven itself."


## A Situation Requiring Great Strength of Heart

In this story about mountain climbing, consider how relentless the ego can be in attempting to keep you enmeshed in suffering, fixated in five-sense reality, unaware of your Soul's journey.

Some years ago, we had the privilege of sitting with someone grieving the loss of his Beloved brother who had chosen to end his own life. The brother, not yet 50, had been a renowned physician and surgeon until a debilitating neurological condition left him physically incapable of practicing medicine. At the time of his diagnosis, he appeared to have made it to "the top" in physical-world reality as a leader in his field. He was wealthy, the owner of several properties, and married with children. He'd achieved multiple measures of success on the Goal Line, only to experience successive losses, each in and of itself difficult to Accept—his health, profession, status, family, and financial resources. When thus presented with challenges on the Goal Line, he sadly did not have the Awareness, information, or tools necessary to assist himself in successfully utilizing these challenges as opportunities for Healing, transformation, and ultimately Awakening.

Our friend, the surviving brother, was suffering greatly. He was deeply hurt and tortured by anger and emotional pain fueled by righteous thoughts. He judged family members and others as ignorant, as standing by and doing nothing to help his brother. And, tormented by a disturbing dream in which his own face was burned away by an accidental encounter with hot tar, he was clearly holding himself culpable as well.

As he shared his pain with us, it became evident that it did not take much to trigger his flash point. Although he was able to carry out his own professional responsibilities in his daily life, he was very reactive, operating on an extremely short fuse. His ego was having a heyday scourging him with brutal thoughts of self-blame and revenge.

We asked him if there was any place of sanctuary where he did not experience the suffering. He reported that he experienced moments of respite and comfort in the Presence of his infant daughter, whose Love was Healing balm. A drop of honey residing within a tiny body—an oasis in the midst of a desert burned barren by anger, judgment, guilt, and shame.

As we listened Compassionately to him, we became aware that while his grief was deeply understandable, the torture that he was experiencing was largely self-inflicted. He strongly identified professionally with the Shaman, the Healer, and it was beginning to dawn on him that he was experiencing the shadow side of that identification through not caring for himself—not bringing Acceptance to his own grief, Self-Compassion to his own pain, and Self-Forgiveness to his own judgments.

After more Heart-Centered Listening, we began to gently, yet directly, reflect to him the arrogance and righteousness of his ego's position of pretending to know what *should* have happened, what others *should* have done, who *should* be assigned blame and righteously punished, and how his brother's death *should* have been avoided. We were aware of how humbling it is for the Shaman, the Healer, to make Peace with the fact that he didn't know—that he was ignorant of how to save or heal his brother. We encouraged him, softly sharing the ancient proverb, "Physician, heal thyself."

We reminded him to look from the altitude of the Soul Line and to consider the alchemical magic of Spirit and the opportunity of nothing less than transmuting this lead produced by the ego. It was an opportunity for Awakening into the Awareness of the Golden Chalice of his Soul—the blessing of drinking of the heavenly nectars of Peace, Joy, and Love in the Golden Temple atop the Mountain of Light. The opportunity was nothing less than surrendering to the Carver's Hands as David Whyte, the poet, so aptly wrote in his poem, "Faces at Braga":

> *If only our own faces*
> *would allow the invisible carver's hand*
> *to bring the deep grain of love to the surface.*

As we completed our conversation, we encouraged our friend to write a Prayer of Gratitude for the gift of his brother and the goodness of his own life. He was climbing his Mountain of Light, and we were grateful to have had the privilege of guiding him, Spiritual Crampons and all, in his ascension to a place of Peace.

### *Climbing the Mountain of Light*

While we were in the middle of writing this book, a woman we've known for many years, whom we love and respect, approached us at an event to ask if she could talk with us about an inner experience she'd had. It had been triggered by the following quote from her Spiritual Teacher John-Roger, which she had contemplated and attempted to live into for more than 45 years—with, in her mind, varying degrees of success. "If you would know the secret of Soul Transcendence, look for the good in people and things, and leave the rest to God."

A librarian by profession, she is also an excellent pianist with an outrageous comedic sense of humor. As part of her own Spiritual practice and quest to actualize the quote for herself, she'd often performed a song she'd written, "Lookin' for the Good in Everything," during many volunteer shows she had done for shut-ins in nursing homes. Set to a calypso beat, the lyrics are:

Chorus:

*I'm lookin' for the good in everything.*
*Lookin' for the good in everything.*
*Lookin' for the good in everything.*
*And all the rest I'm leavin' to God.*

Verse:

*Sometimes I don't feel too hot.*
*(Backup singers: Not Hot!)*
*Sometimes I don't feel too cool.*
*(Backup singers: Not Cool!)*
*Sometimes I don't know just what to do.*
*So here's how I get through.*

Chorus:

*I'm lookin' for the good in everything.*
*Lookin' for the good in everything.*
*Lookin' for the good in everything.*
*And all the rest I'm leavin' to God.*

Then, one day, while she contemplated the quote from John-Roger, something suddenly and spontaneously opened up in the center of her head. In her words:

*Instantly and effortlessly my perception changed. I experienced myself being something on the order of a mile high. I was in an ecstasy and was receiving a transmission of Divine Love and Light. I experienced that I exist in multidimensions, including dimensions that are normally closed to my perception—dimensions that are many levels, that are much subtler, yet are much greater and more true than my "ordinary" senses are able to perceive. I experienced myself as much richer, deeper, truer, more wonderful than I had ever imagined. And I experienced myself being part of something on the order of "the Almighty."*

*The Light was vibrating, giving off the most exquisite tones and sounds that were multidimensional and that conveyed a vitality of the life force. I experienced a revelation of my Authentic Self, and it was good. I felt this Light was Healing my body, mind, and emotions.*

*I asked inwardly, "What is this?"*

*Something or someone said, "This is the Koh-i-Noor."*

*I had heard of Koh-i-Noor as a mystery school, and I'd heard of it as a diamond, a piece of jewelry. But this Koh-i-Noor was a new meaning. I knew beyond any doubt that the Koh-i-Noor as a Mountain of Light is part of every human being. I was filled with Gratitude that Spirit saw fit to give me the gift of this Awareness, even for a short time.*

*I leaned into the experience. I repeated the essence of the quote silently. "I am looking for the good. I am looking for the good."*

*Gradually my Awareness shifted to the "I am" part of the quote. I AM looking for the good. The "I am" became charged, and I was more Awake to it than I can ever remember. I heard myself repeating inwardly, "I am, I AM, I AM." In so doing, I became even more Awake. It was a glorious experience.*

*After a while, my "ordinary world" with my ordinary perceptions returned. However, some recollection of the Koh-i-Noor has stayed with me. The "I am" stayed with me more than before. It is still present as a comforter in times of trouble and as an inspiration in times of seeking to Awaken—to know my Authentic Self.*

May you bring forward your Strength of Heart, step into your Spiritual Crampons, and receive the Blessings of perseverance, resilience, clarity of intention, inner commitment, and humor necessary to sustain yourself in Awakening into the Awareness that as you climb the Mountain of Light, you are steadily climbing into nothing less than the Awareness that *you* are that Presence of Love and *you* are the Mountain of Light.

Are you ready? Let's strap on our Spiritual Crampons and continue this grand adventure!

## THIS CHAPTER'S PRACTICES

### *Grit and Spiritual Crampons*

We invite you to write in your journal, exploring your responses to the following questions about strapping on your Spiritual Crampons and bringing forward Grit—demonstrating your ability to sustain interest and engagement, and consciously participating in your Awakening. For the lifelong process of Awakening requires perseverance, resilience, optimism, intention, and commitment.

- What strengths do you see yourself demonstrating in terms of willingness to demonstrate Grit, the commitment and endurance to participate lifelong in your conscious Awakening?

- In what ways are you demonstrating, or have you already demonstrated, these attitudes and qualities in your personal and/or professional life?

- What present opportunities do you perceive as challenging you to stand forward, strapping on your Spiritual Crampons and bringing forth your clarity of intention, your Strength of Heart, your commitment—bottom line, your Grit?

- What are some small steps you can take, if you choose to, in support of more fully demonstrating Grit in the process of your Awakening?

## *Gratitude List*

Make a list of at least 10 "things"—people, experiences, qualities within yourself, etc.—for which you are Grateful, and then write a Prayer of Gratitude.

## *Gratitude Prayer*

At both the beginning and completion of your day, you have a wonderful opportunity for offering a spontaneous prayer of Gratitude, if for no other reason than that you are alive and Aware of the Spiritual Blessings of Awakening into the Loving that you are. (For myself [Mary], I love moving into the yoga posture of Child's Pose when I offer my prayer of Gratitude.)

---

### INTENTION

I am demonstrating Grit and Gratitude as I move through my everyday life, using the resources and the tools I am learning as Spiritual Crampons whenever and wherever I encounter opportunities for Awakening into the True Gold of my Authentic Self—Remembering the Light Within.

---

# CHAPTER 26

# LIVING A SOUL-CENTERED LIFE

*"Tomorrow is a new day . . . begin it well and serenely, and with too high a spirit to be cumbered with your old nonsense."*
— RALPH WALDO EMERSON

What is the real story of Awakening as you live into the Awareness that you truly are a Divine Being having a human experience?

What happens as you integrate Seeing the Loving Essence and Heart-Centered Listening and they become a Way of Being?

What transpires when you catch on to the fact that life is happening inside your consciousness? When you realize that your experience in physical-world reality is determined largely by the beliefs found within the matrix of your perceptual filter, functioning as your internal operating system . . . and you consciously begin downloading and installing a software upgrade?

What shifts occur when you realize you are the architect of your life, and that your inner and outer choices are the building blocks of your future . . . and you begin making more Self-Honoring choices, choices more in harmony with your Loving nature and your Soul's Purpose?

What happens when you wake up to the Authentic Empowerment available through taking responsibility for your judgments and upsets with the intention of releasing them . . . and you begin realizing you are at cause rather than at the effect?

What happens when you begin reaching for the Write and Burn paper when upset is triggered inside of you rather than judging and blaming the person you used to perceive as the cause of your upset . . . and you experientially discover that you can truly release your upsets, that they can actually dissolve into the nothingness from which they came?

What happens when you begin to apply Loving to the places inside where there is hurt . . . and you actually engage in Compassionate Self-Forgiveness of your judgments, misinterpretations, and misidentifications—and you let them go?

What happens when you begin catching on that listening to K-EGO is not good for your health, happiness, and well-being . . . and you change stations to K-L♥VE?

What happens when the deep wellspring of Compassion that resides within your Authentic Self begins Flowing abundantly through you . . . and you *wake up* into the Awareness that you are Love?

Here's what happens! You've struck it rich! This is when life truly begins, for in those moments of Revelation, *you know* the Mother Lode, the Source of True Gold, is within you—in fact, it *is* you! You've experienced your Authentic Self, and your Awakening Heart is aware of the download of Spirit's Blessing through you as you.

Through involving yourself with the material in this book and participating in the Practices and Intentions, you are discovering what it means to *Remember* and live into the fullness of the Love that is inside of you . . . to live a life of Meaning, Purpose, and Fulfillment . . . a Soul-Centered Life. It is the experience of Awakening into the Awareness of who you truly are and living your life from within that Awakened state.

Your consciousness becomes a conduit for Living Love and your course through life, an expression of that Love—for you *know*, as poet Rod McKuen knew: "It doesn't matter who you love or how you love, but that you love." To which we would add—*for you are Love*!

Remember that growth is a process, not an event. We support and encourage you! The Principles and Practices of Spiritual Psychology are practical tools you can use each and every day of your life in service to your Awakening.

Strap on your Spiritual Crampons and join in as we continue climbing the Mountain of Light, nourished and supported by the Wellspring of Loving that springs eternal in your Spiritual Heart.

## THIS CHAPTER'S PRACTICE

### *Moving Forward into Soul-Centered Living*

You've read the book. You've experienced the Principles and Practices of Spiritual Psychology in action through using each chapter's Practices as stepping-stones in your Awakening. For this chapter's Practice, we invite you to open the book to any page and engage in one of the Practices you find therein.

Alternatively, you can browse the table of contents and select a chapter to review, choosing Practices you can use based on what's currently unfolding within you. Perhaps you feel moved to participate in a random act of kindness. Perhaps what's present is an opportunity to engage in Writing and Burning and Compassionate Self-Forgiveness to help clear up something that's bothering you. Perhaps you become inspired by a journaling prompt. Practice Accepting whatever comes forward for you in the moment as the right one for you when considered from within your Spiritual Context. Remember, you're a Divine Being *having* and *using* a human experience for the purpose of Awakening into the Awareness that you are the Presence of Love.

## INTENTION

I am living my life in ways that foster my Awakening, residing in my Authentic Self more and more of the time, experiencing the Fulfillment and Peace of Knowing that I am at Home in the Heart of God. I am Joyfully Singing my Soul's Song, Remembering the Light Within!

# AFTERWORD

Have you ever experienced an electrical power outage in the evening—one that called you to light a candle in a room filled with darkness? Occasionally, when my (Mary's) family was summering at our cottage on a beautiful remote lake in northern Wisconsin, there were fierce thunderstorms and the incandescent lights would go out, sometimes for several hours. There were no streetlights, so the darkness of night enveloped the cottage. It happened often enough that my parents had an ample supply of white candles close at hand.

I actually loved those experiences, as there was something deeply intimate, a kind of Communion that took place among us as we sat together in the candlelight. Sometimes we played a children's card game, sometimes we drank hot chocolate, sometimes my father told us a story, and sometimes we simply sat together in the Silence, listening to the rain on the roof.

Perhaps like me, you appreciate the Peaceful Illumination that radiates from a single lighted candle. In those moments, darkness recedes in the face of Luminous Light. Now, consider the Beauty, Brilliance, and Radiance that emanate as a single human being courageously stands forth in the Loving, fulfilling their purpose, sharing the Glory of their Light, their Love, their Gifts, and their

Joy. This reminds and inspires me to also stand forth and share the Radiant Light and Loving of my Heart and Soul.

Similarly, have you ever fallen asleep in a dark room, nurtured into the Awareness of the Peace and Love within the hearth of your Heart by the warmth and flickering flames of a fireplace fire? The experiences and expressions of Loving are abundant and ever present. Your experiences on this earth are designed for Awakening into the Awareness of your Self as an emanation, a radiation, an expression of Living Love! They are intended to be vehicles for your En*light*enment fostering you in Remembering the Light Within.

Remaining cloaked within the veil of forgetfulness results in unconscious living characterized by experiences of impoverishment, lack, disconnection, conflict, separation, estrangement, unhappiness, and unworthiness, which mask Awareness of the human Heart and the human Spirit. To be asleep is to obscure the Radiance of your Loving Heart.

As more and more people Awaken, what's next? When I (Ron) consider that question, it always reminds me of a time several years ago when we were facilitating a weeklong lab in Spiritual Psychology. The format involved 10 participants in four rooms, and each room had a room facilitator to guide the work.

Since these labs are the culmination of a two-year Spiritual Psychology Program, participants often go very deep within their consciousness. In one session where I was the room facilitator, one young woman was sharing her pain about the state of the world and all the pain and suffering that exists on the planet. The most painful aspect she shared had to do with the question she had often asked: "If there's a God, why does He allow so much suffering?"

I thought for a minute and softly said, "Well, if you were God, what would you do?"

The woman stopped her crying for a moment and replied, "Well, if I were God, I'd send an Angel to bring Light into the darkness."

I paused, and then softly said, "Well, now you know what your job is."

Waking up into the Awareness of your Loving ushers you into the Spiritual Context, into living life in Communion with your Essential Spiritual Nature. As Buddha said, "Thousands of candles can be lit from a single candle, and the life of the candle will not be shortened." We add, "The more you share your Loving, the more Awake and Aware you become, and the more you inspire others into their Awakening."

You have our Love, support, and encouragement in Awakening and living into the fullness of the Loving that is inside of you. Your candle is lit! As you reflect on this book, consider the following intention.

*I am a Lighthouse of Living Love—Awake and Aware—sharing Radiant Light, Luminous Loving, Peace, and Joy with all people and in all situations for the Highest Good of All Concerned.*

In your Authentic Self, you're already Awake to the Love that you are! This book is intended as both inspiration and support for you in Remembering the Light Within, for that Light is truly what You are and by Shining it, you assist in the Enlightenment of all.

— Mary & Ron Hulnick

✦ ✦ ✦

# APPENDIX A

## The 33 Principles of Spiritual Psychology

1.  God is everything in existence, both seen and unseen.

2.  The nature of God is Love.

3.  Since we are all a part of God, our Essential Nature also is Love—and we have the opportunity of *knowing* our Loving Nature experientially, Here and Now.

4.  We are not human beings with Souls; we are Souls *using* a human experience for the purpose of Awakening.

5.  Earth functions as a school for Spiritual Awakening, meaning Conscious Awareness of Principles #2 and #3 (above). Everyone registers for their specific Curriculum.

6.  Physical-world reality exists for the purpose of Spiritual Awakening; thus, life is for learning and growing spiritually.

7.  Graduation is based upon mastering your lessons, resulting in Wisdom and Compassion.

8. Everyone has the potential, resources, and destiny to graduate. There is no failure—only repeated opportunity.

9. Everyone will graduate. The only real variable is time, and the only real time is Now.

10. Your primary goal is not to change the school; your primary goal is to graduate.

11. Awakening is a process, not an event.

12. Awakening can be accelerated by learning and implementing the Principles and Practices of Spiritual Psychology.

13. Your Spiritual Curriculum consists of unresolved issues as well as opportunities for service, sharing your gifts, and living into your Heartfelt dreams.

14. An unresolved issue is anything that disturbs your Peace.

15. Unresolved issues are not bad; they're simply part of your Spiritual Curriculum.

16. Unresolved issues are blessings, as they are opportunities for Healing and Awakening.

17. Accepting personal responsibility for your Spiritual Curriculum is empowering and opens the door to Freedom.

18. Nothing outside of you *causes* your disturbances.

19. All "becauses"—i.e., anything that disturbs your Peace—is, in Spiritual Reality, a trigger to an unresolved issue that is part of your Spiritual Curriculum, providing an opportunity for true Healing.

20. Outer experience is a reflection of inner reality.

21. Personal internal reality is subjective. Therefore, what you believe determines your experience.

22. Experiences you judge, you attract. They tend to proliferate, repeat, and multiply.

23. You create your future by how you respond to your experiences now.

24. There are no mistakes—only opportunities for Learning, Healing, and Awakening unto Love.

25. How you relate to an issue *is* the issue; or, how you relate with yourself while you go through an issue *is* the issue.

26. Healing is the application of Loving to the places inside that hurt or suffer, or Healing is the "Flooding with Loving" of all the places inside that hurt or suffer—thereby dissolving them.

27. In your Universe, your word is your law; thus, the power of intention.

28. The mind is a tool to be used in service to the Heart.

29. Maintaining supportive disciplines is a demonstration of Self-Loving.

30. Intimacy is a natural and *automatic* by-product of honest, caring Self-expression.

31. Judgment is self-condemnation; Self-Forgiveness is restoration; and Compassion, Acceptance, Peace, and Joy naturally follow.

32. Loving, Healing, Awakening, and Evolving are all the same process whereby you experience deeper and deeper Awareness of your Essential Nature we refer to as your Authentic Self—already fully present and characterized by Unconditional Loving, Wisdom, Joy, Peace, Creativity, Compassion, Happiness, and more.

33. A life lived in Acceptance is a life devoid of unnecessary emotional suffering. It's a life filled with Love.

❖ ❖ ❖

# APPENDIX B

## The Process for Developing Rating Scales

Rating Scales are best utilized when you are working with subjective types of experience that do not readily lend themselves to objective tracking. In other words, Rating Scales are a method of quantifying your subjective experience for the purposes of your own personal experimentation.

The purpose of using Rating Scales is as support in transforming patterns in behavior and consciousness so you have a way of assessing the degree to which you are coming more in alignment with the experience that you would like to have. Both the use of Rating Scales *and* the process of creating them can serve as powerful instruments for facilitating positive movement, Healing, and transformation in consciousness.

For example, you might like to experience yourself moving from the experience of despair or depression into Joy, from anger and "I'm upset because . . ." to Inner Peace, from self-betrayal to Self-Honoring Choices, or from withholding to Authentic Self-Expression. Or perhaps you intend to experience enhanced levels of Intimacy or Good Humor. Always, your intention is that of guiding yourself along a continuum from less preferred to more preferred experiences.

Often, the very process of simply constructing a Rating Scale is a way of gaining altitude and perspective and can result in greater

Awareness, clarity, optimism, and positive change. Because you can utilize the Rating Scale to track experience, the very act of tracking is an act of observing. This is important since the very act of observing brings that which you are observing into focus; in and of itself, this can be a Healing action.

An effective Rating Scale will typically include ratings of 1 through 9, with 1 being the lowest rating and 9 being the highest. Constructing a scale in this way provides a definite midpoint, and also provides sufficient range for whatever you are rating to have sufficient dimension within which it can move.

### *Constructing a Rating Scale:*

1)   Begin by selecting an area or dimension of your experience within which you want to create change. Describe the qualities and characteristics of your current experience.

2)   Write a statement that describes what you would experience if the dimension or quality of experience were to deteriorate somewhat. This will be point number 1 on a 9-point rating scale. (Thus, you will be allowing a lot of space for upward movement.)

3)   Write a statement describing your Ideal Scene for your experience within this dimension. Bring in the qualities of a living vision of the experience. This will be point number 9 on the scale.

4)   Read over the statements for point number 1 and point number 9 and determine, as best as possible, what would describe a midpoint. This will be point number 5 on the scale and will constitute a turning point at which the scale shifts from negative to positive. Point 5 will be an essentially neutral statement.

5)   Now read over the statements for point number 1 and point number 5 and determine, as best as possible, what would describe the midpoint between points 1 and 5. This will be point number 3 on the scale. Similarly, read over the statements for

point number 5 and point number 9 and create an appropriate description for point 7.

6) Repeat this process for points 2, 4, 6, and 8, so that all points on the scale have been described. Keep statements simple. Remember that images and metaphors can be effective.

7) As a check, if this has been done effectively, the original statement describing the current state of the dimension should show up as either point number 2 or 3, thus providing lots of potential for upward movement in the course of time.

Now ask the following questions about your rating scale so as to evaluate its effectiveness:

- Is it valid? This is another way of asking whether upward movement along the dimension you have developed and which you will be tracking represents an important element toward successful completion of your project.

- Does it have consistency? Do the intervals appear to be as equally spaced as possible? In other words, is there a gradual increase in the scale as it moves from 1 to 9, and do the jumps from one number to the next seem to be about the same?

# Examples of Rating Scales

## MAKING SELF-HONORING CHOICES:
### Daily Rating Scale

1.  I make choices that abandon my own needs and do what others want so they'll love me. I experience significant deple- tion as a result. I don't want to be here, I don't belong here, I'm lonely, and I can't cope. What good am I? Who cares? No one. I'm on my own case—so what's new? This is all I deserve, and nothing will ever change. God has left me here and is punishing me.

2.  I joylessly plod on the wheel of life. I'm tired, and life is a drag. I don't see the point, and I'm certainly not going to ask for help. Frankly, I don't have the energy to help myself, or others. No one wants to hang around me (big surprise)—and I don't want to deal with other people's egos anyway. Still, I'm afraid of being alone, so I swallow my resentment. I'm not important, even to me—much less God.

3.  I tell others "yes" when I clearly mean "no," and then I'm irritable because I am not getting what I need out of these situations. I'm willing to forego my own needs being met to maintain homeostasis in a relationship. I'm unable, or unwill- ing, to risk standing up for myself, or asking for what I want. God helps those who help themselves? Oh, I'll cope somehow, probably, but my life doesn't matter much.

4.  I'm still making "nice" and avoiding situations where I feel challenged to speak my truth. I compromise for the sake of maintaining relationships, saying to myself, "Don't rock the boat—it's nothing, no big deal." I keep the peace and hide my true feelings, but I'm aware that I'm doing this. Maybe I should pray.

5.  I am beginning to have a sense of what my own needs are and occasionally make self-caring choices. I'm feeling neither sup- ported nor abandoned by others, and I'm beginning to see that my life has some value. I find myself having more energy. I

can accept myself as I am at times. I realize others may actually like me. Life is still hard, but with effort, I'm managing. Maybe God hears my prayers.

6.  I can now see how to set boundaries and support myself—and I'm starting to do that. I'm not always graceful or easy or comfortable, but I'm worth it, and I sense that others may respect and enjoy me more. Sometimes I backpedal when challenged, or feel embarrassed, and that's okay. Life can be good; people are good. And God is okay with me.

7.  More and more I hold clear boundaries, and easily and lovingly say no to that which does not work for me. I am gentle and supportive of myself, and my needs are getting met! When tested, I stand up and say what's true for me. Speaking up in support of myself, or for what I perceive is the Highest Good, empowers me, even if it feels a little risky. I give, I receive, I enjoy life, and I know God loves me.

8.  I am clear about how to support myself fully, and I love knowing I'm worth it. Other people are seeing my strength and clarity, and find me attractive. I speak honestly and from my Heart, and I now know how to be good to myself and to others at the same time. I enjoy taking risks when it's appropriate. Life is Joyful. I love my Self and God.

9.  I am whole and complete in all that I am. My choices reflect the depth of my Self-Care and Self-Love, and I'm filled with energy and enthusiasm for my life. I belong to my life, I belong to my Self, and in Joy, I belong to Spirit. I connect with others easily and naturally, in ways we enjoy. My life is flowing beautifully. I am deeply fulfilled in this new way of being with myself. The abundance of God's Loving radiates in me and through me, and I am grateful!

## AUTHENTIC SELF-EXPRESSION:
### Daily Rating Scale

1.  I don't have anything of value to share with others. I feel terrified and I know that it's not safe to share my Authentic Self, and I don't even know what that is. I'm judging myself.

2.  I can't think of anything that I have of value to share with others. I'm very afraid of rejection, so I keep quiet. I keep my Authentic Self hidden. I'm aware that I'm judging myself.

3.  I have something I'd like to share that is important to me, but I am afraid of rejection. I start to express myself authentically, but I stop the expression due to my fear and discomfort. I'm aware that I'm judging myself and I do Compassionate Self-Forgiveness.

4.  I have something I'd like to share that is important to me, but I am afraid of rejection. I take a risk and express myself authentically, and I feel embarrassed. I am glad that I took the risk even though it feels very scary. I have to be very careful about who I share myself with. I'm aware that I'm judging myself and I do Compassionate Self-Forgiveness.

5.  I have something I'd like to share that is important to me, even though I am uneasy about expressing my authenticity. I am glad that I took the risk even though it feels very uncomfortable. I am worried about what others think, but I choose to be authentic anyway. I'm aware that I'm judging myself and I do Compassionate Self-Forgiveness.

6.  I am daring to share myself authentically with others and getting more comfortable with the idea of expressing my thoughts and feelings. It still requires a lot of courage and I'm aware that I feel embarrassed. I'm judging myself and I do Compassionate Self-Forgiveness.

7.  I am willing to share myself authentically with others and okay with the idea of expressing my thoughts and feelings. I'm aware that it requires conscious effort and is not natural, graceful, or easy. I am still concerned about others' reactions, but

I know I am not responsible for their feelings. I immediately forgive myself for any judgments, even though they are not as present.

8.  I am willing to share myself authentically with others and I enjoy expressing my thoughts and feelings. I am feeling comfortable with myself and am not concerned about the reactions of others.

9.  I am joyfully and naturally expressing my Authentic Self with ease and grace. I am happily expressing my Authentic Self.

## SEEING MYSELF AS A FUN-LOVING AND JOYFUL PERSON:
### Daily Rating Scale

1. When I try to be funny, people stare. I decide I am not funny and will never try to be funny again. There is no such thing as Joy.

2. When other people are funny, I realize I'm not and judge the hell out of myself about that. I doubt that I could be a Joyful person. Ever.

3. Once in a while, I try to be funny. It's a lot of work, and it is anything but fun. I have seen Joy in other people, but it's not for me.

4. I'm surprised—people were laughing with me, and I was laughing, and it wasn't hard. It's rare, but I'm clear: This could be fun! I can see a glimmer of Joy in myself.

5. Fun is showing up! I go there more often, and it feels fun! I have had a few experiences of Joy.

6. I catch myself having fun, and being lighthearted, and see that it is just me being me. I'm a fun person. I'm having more spontaneous experiences of Joy in my life.

7. I see lots of natural opportunities for fun. I hear "I think you're fun!" and I am not even startled by this self-concept. I love being around Joyful people and I'm expressing my Joy more often.

8. My Humor and sense of fun spring forward naturally as I go through the day. I realize: "Hey, I'm a fun person!" I'm Joyful a lot of the time. Life is good!

9. I realize I can genuinely challenge Jay Leno for his job. He talks fast, but I am funnier! I am a Joyful Presence in the world!

# ACKNOWLEDGMENTS

We're deeply grateful to all the wonderful people who have supported us in writing *Remembering the Light Within.* Thank you to:

All the courageous graduates of the University of Santa Monica, whose willingness to enter the Spiritual Context and dedication to Awakening have touched our hearts, inspired our vision, and helped us chart and navigate the ever-expanding frontiers of Spiritual Psychology.

Licia Rester-Frazee and Mike Murphy, who heard me (Mary) when I said I wanted to write for more people, and not only encouraged me but also assisted me in lightening my load so that I could devote time to creating *33 Days of Awakening*, a prelude to writing this book.

Arianna Huffington, for her vision and inspiration in offering *33 Days of Awakening* to a worldwide audience through *The Huffington Post.*

Agapi Stassinopolous, for her Loving, encouragement, and tangible support in ways that truly made a difference.

Our personal editor, Angela Renkoski, whose enthusiasm for this material and keen attention to detail helped guide us through the wild, wild West that constitutes the terrain of authoring a book from inception to completion.

Nancy O'Leary, for her gracious willingness, Love, support, and meticulous attention to the final page proofs.

Lenore Perry, for her brilliant creative vision and beautiful execution of the cover design.

Everyone on the faculty and staff of the University of Santa Monica, who believed in us, supported us, and generously put their Love and gifts into this work.

Reid Tracy, for so enthusiastically giving us this opportunity, along with members of the Hay House team, including Nicolette Salamanca Young for her patience, attention to detail, and significant contributions to the book's completed form; Melanie Bell for her helpful feedback; Anne Barthel for her wisdom in all matters and inspirations about the title; and Patty Gift for her kind support.

Robert Holden, for his Love, support, wise counsel, and friendship.

Corinne Burchett and Peggy Bularz, for being the Presence of Love in our lives.

Renée Adams, for holding the Light and managing a myriad of details, helping free us to write.

Michael Hayes, for his Presence and constancy of Love and friendship all these years.

Our feline friends, Darling Isabella, aka Baby Ummms, and Beloved Theresa, our companions throughout this adventure, providing continuous purrs and adorable antics by way of Love and support.

Spirit, for Loving, supporting, guiding, and inspiring us throughout this process.

And John-Roger, your Loving support has made all the difference. Thank you, J-R, for assisting us in Remembering the Light within our selves as well as the Light within all people, and as you would say, "regardless of race, creed, color, situation, circumstance, or environment."

❖ ❖ ❖

# ABOUT THE AUTHORS

Drs. Ron and Mary Hulnick are recognized worldwide as pioneers and leaders in the field of Spiritual Psychology™ and as Master Teachers and Facilitators of Awakening in Consciousness. Together they have played a seminal role in the development of the study and practice of Spiritual Psychology at the University of Santa Monica (USM) since its inception in 1981. As USM's Founding Faculty and Co-Directors of the University of Santa Monica, they designed the University's life-changing Programs, and they continue to serve as executive faculty.

Ron and Mary Hulnick designed the University's experiential educational programs, which are provided within a Soul-Centered learning environment that nurtures the Awakening of the human Spirit inherent in each student. Their vision and intention has always been to provide students with practical information, tools, and experiences for transforming their consciousness and their lives. The hallmarks of this educational process are that it is engaging, relevant, meaningful, supportive, inspiring, practical, nurturing, and, ultimately, transformational. USM graduates around the world share that being with Ron and Mary in the classroom is, without exception, one of the most transformative, Loving, and memorable experiences that they will cherish for a lifetime.

The Hulnicks are the Executive Producers of the University's award-winning documentary *Freedom to Choose*, which took first place at the 2009 Emerging Filmmaker Showcase at the Cannes Film Festival. Their book *Loyalty to Your Soul: The Heart of Spiritual Psychology* has been described by Caroline Myss as a "stunning masterpiece of primary importance."

Ron and Mary are both licensed Marriage and Family Therapists, and Mary is also a licensed Clinical Psychologist. They have been happily married for 38 years and reside with their beloved feline friends—Isabella, aka Baby Ummms, and Theresa—in the greater Los Angeles area.

*Websites:* www.universityofsantamonica.edu and www.usmonline.org

✦ ✦ ✦

We hope you enjoyed this Hay House book. If you'd like to receive our online catalog featuring additional information on Hay House books and products, or if you'd like to find out more about the Hay Foundation, please contact:

Hay House, Inc., P.O. Box 5100, Carlsbad, CA 92018-5100
(760) 431-7695 or (800) 654-5126
(760) 431-6948 (fax) or (800) 650-5115 (fax)
www.hayhouse.com® • www.hayfoundation.org

✤ ✤ ✤

***Published and distributed in Australia by:***
Hay House Australia Pty. Ltd., 18/36 Ralph St., Alexandria NSW 2015
*Phone:* 612-9669-4299 • *Fax:* 612-9669-4144 • www.hayhouse.com.au

***Published and distributed in the United Kingdom by:***
Hay House UK, Ltd., Astley House, 33 Notting Hill Gate, London W11 3JQ
*Phone:* 44-20-3675-2450 • *Fax:* 44-20-3675-2451 • www.hayhouse.co.uk

***Published and distributed in the Republic of South Africa by:***
Hay House SA (Pty), Ltd., P.O. Box 990, Witkoppen 2068
info@hayhouse.co.za • www.hayhouse.co.za

***Published in India by:*** Hay House Publishers India,
Muskaan Complex, Plot No. 3, B-2, Vasant Kunj, New Delhi 110 070
*Phone:* 91-11-4176-1620 • *Fax:* 91-11-4176-1630 • www.hayhouse.co.in

***Distributed in Canada by:***
Raincoast Books, 2440 Viking Way, Richmond, B.C. V6V 1N2
*Phone:* 1-800-663-5714 • *Fax:* 1-800-565-3770 • www.raincoast.com

✤ ✤ ✤

Take Your Soul on a Vacation

Visit www.HealYourLife.com® to regroup, recharge, and reconnect
with your own magnificence. Featuring blogs, mind-body-spirit news,
and life-changing wisdom from Louise Hay and friends.

Visit www.HealYourLife.com today!

# NOTES